Leave No Soul Behind

A Catholic Handbook

✝
Leave No
Soul Behind
A Catholic Handbook

Fred Vilbig

Imprimatur and Nihil Obstat

In accordance with CIC 827, permission to publish has been granted on
June 23, 2020, by the Most Reverend Mark S. Rivituso, Auxiliary Bishop of St. Louis.
Permission to publish is an indication that nothing contrary to Church teaching is
contained in this particular work. It does not imply any endorsement of the
opinions expressed in the publication, or a general endorsement of any
author; nor is any liability assumed by this permission.

Book Design by Cathryn Vilbig

Cover Image: *Ascension of Christ* by Pietro Perugino (†1500), Musee des Beaux Arts de Lyon.
This is the central panel of an altarpiece commissioned by the Benedictine monastery in
Perugia, Italy. It was designed along a vertical and a horizontal axis: vertically from earth to
Heaven, with the Blessed Virgin, Jesus (surrounded by angels), and God the Father (in a lunette
above this image); and horizontally, with the Apostles, St. Paul, and other early Church figures.
It was at the Ascension that Jesus gave us the Great Commission.

ISBN: 978-1-7358403-0-7

Dedication

*I do a lot of reading, writing, and talking
about our Catholic faith. One night at a parish fish fry,
one of our deacons asked my wife, Diane, if she read a lot
as well, and she said that she did not. That is true,
but it is not really the complete truth.*

*You see, I talk the faith, but my wife lives it. She has
always been much more patient and loving with our
children than I ever have. She has lovingly and devotedly
taken care of her parents as they aged, and our kids
will tell you that was not always easy. And the
hardest cross of all, she married me.*

*I can never repay her for all that she has done
for me, our family, or her family, but I dedicate
this book to her, as feeble as that might be.*

Table of Contents

I am just a layman. Although I do have a degree in philosophy, I have no advanced degrees in theology. I am not a minister of the Church in any official capacity. I am just a lay Catholic trying to live my faith.

This Handbook is the product of a talk that I gave several years ago. I was asked by St. Joseph Evangelization Network to speak at a local parish during Lent. The topic I was given was the "battle for souls." Having eleven children of my own, this is a very personal topic for me. I spoke about things that the Church has taught for centuries, but today that message is relatively muted, if not silenced. People seem to have forgotten a lot of the traditions that grew up in the Church over the centuries. The talk was well received, and some people suggested that I should do something more on the topic.

What I have written in this Handbook should be taken as my prayerful reflections on what we as Catholics are facing and what we can do about it. My legal training tells me that I should base my statements on precedent or authority of some sort. In our faith, the greatest precedents we have are the Church, the Bible (which by the grace of God is the product of the Church), and the Saints.[1] Although I have tried to remain faithful to the revelation of Jesus Christ through His Church, I do not want to lead anyone astray. If there is something that I have written that

---

1 Throughout this Handbook, I will distinguish between "Saints" who have been canonized by the Church, and "saints" who are the holy people who make up the Body of Christ, but have not been officially recognized by the Church – hopefully all of us.

is contrary to any of those sources, please disregard it. My only hope, my only purpose here, is to bring people, both my readers and those with whom they come in contact, closer to God.

In your charity, please pray for me and my family, as I will for you and yours.

Preface

The beginning premise of this book is the statement, 'the world is a mess.' I believe this to be so, and I point the finger at us. All of us. As St. Paul says, we do what we ought not to do, and we don't do what we ought to do.[2]

The problems in our society seem enormous and beyond the ability of any individual to fix, but I think many good and faithful Catholics want to do something. They feel called to do something. And we are not powerless. God has a purpose, a mission, for each one of us. The faithful Christian is called to live their faith in deep and profound ways. The laity are members of the Church Militant, and this is the spiritual battle we are called to fight.

Many of these ideas are foreign to contemporary Catholics, but they are as old as the Church itself, if not even older, going back to the time of Abraham. In my experience, the church has stopped proclaiming them in recent times. Or if they haven't completely stopped, some of the Church's current ministers have de-emphasized them. By this Handbook, I want to suggest

---

2 Romans 7:15

that we should return to these fundamental practices: deep and reflective prayer; following the lives of the Saints, who have so much to teach us; and taking up the cross and leading a life of sacrifice.

This Handbook is designed to give faithful Catholics some ideas and suggest some practices about how we can more devoutly live our faith.

The first section is a statement of the case. Whenever I write as a lawyer, I have to start by explaining what I'm going to talk about and why it's important. That is the Conflict.

The second section is an admonishment to pray and pray often, because it is fundamental to our relationship with God. Prayer is the starting point.

The next section talks about how we live our faith, that is, holiness. Holiness is a scary word for a lot of people today, but in my mind, it only means selfless love, the love Jesus showed us in becoming man and dying for us so that we could be with him in Heaven forever.

Finally, there is sacrifice. As I explain, Jesus was emphatic that the Cross was not an option. Each of us in our particular circumstance is called to it every day.

I end this Handbook with a call to action.

We live in dark times. Selfishness and sin seem to pervade everything. This Handbook is a battle cry for action -- but it is a spiritual battle. The stakes are enormous. This is not just a theoretical discussion; rather it is a call to action for the eternal salvation of all of our loved ones and for the world we live in. Nothing could be more important.

PART ONE

The Conflict

Or, A Statement of the Case

The Great Commission

Roughly two thousand years ago, a young man spoke to the eleven companions who circled around Him, uncertain and afraid. To them he said:

All authority in Heaven and on earth has been given to me. Go, therefore, and make disciples of all nations, baptizing them in the name of the Father, and of the Son, and of the Holy Spirit, teaching them to observe all that I have commanded you. And behold, I am with you always, until the end of the age."[3]

That young man, only in his thirties, on the cusp of ascending into Heaven to sit at the right hand of His heavenly Father, charged His apostles to go and make disciples of all nations. He promised He would be with them always, even to the end of time.

It is this promise and admonition which serves as the foundation of the Catholic Church. Go and make disciples of the nations ....

It is an awesome responsibility, hardly understandable in its majesty. Jesus, through his words, challenged us to bring His message to all peoples on this earth. Wrapping us in the mantle of His care, He promised to be with us, to the very end of the age.

His message, His charge, seems abundantly clear: take the Word of God to all. The Word is the truth of His Father, the first person of the Trinity, the Being who caused all that we know to exist. It is He Who brought us into being, and Who imbues us both with His love, and a powerful responsibility.

3 Matthew 28:18-20

How do we do this? The task stuns with its magnitude. How does one spread the word of God? Is our language enough? Our example of living? Our compassion? The strengths of our belief in God?

It seems clear that it is all of these things ... and more. As mere people, we have very little power. Even our steadfast beliefs waver, our lifestyles wander a crooked path. We strive for compassion, but our compassion often lacks fulsomeness. Our language, though undergirded by the Holy Spirit, is often a whisper, not a shout. We, alone, are not enough.

What then do we do?

We look to the words of St. Catherine of Siena: "Be who God meant you to be, and you will set the world on fire."

The World is a Mess

The world is a mess. Everyone is fighting in Washington. There are mass shootings and terrorist attacks. War seems ever present. Radical states are developing nuclear weapons. The third world starves while the wealth gap looms as a global moral failure. Peril casts a pall over the American system of democracy. Families are broken by divorce and abuse. There are seemingly endless scandals in the Church. And it seems that our society produces a lot of shallow narcissists.

It doesn't matter if we are liberal or conservative; Protestant or Catholic; an agnostic, an atheist, or a believer. Everyone agrees that the world is a mess. It may be the only thing that almost everyone can agree on. Yes, the world is a mess, and it doesn't seem to be getting any better. In fact, if anything, it seems to be getting worse.

But that is where the agreement ends. Once we start talking about the causes, the fighting starts. Some will blame too much government; others will blame not enough government. Some will blame big business, and others will blame all of the people without a strong work drive or business ethic. Some will blame the older generation who just don't "get it," while others will blame the younger generation who don't respect tradition. Some will blame the lack of religion, and others will blame religion itself. It's hard to know the truth about the dysfunctions of our society.[4]

If we are completely honest with ourselves, we have to admit that something's not working.

Worldly Solutions Fail

So if everyone knows that things are a mess, what are people doing about it?

I think there are a lot of people who are just overwhelmed. Seeking distraction, they fill up their lives with movies, TV, music, sports, and social events. Others try to numb themselves with alcohol or drugs. It's as if they are trying to hide from the chaos around them. Still others take a blind, apathetic view of their responsibility. They want to live in a bubble or a cocoon. But they are deluding themselves. Hiding from a problem doesn't make it go away.

Some people think they can fix the problems through politics, but even our Founding Fathers knew that alone didn't work. John Adams, one of the signers of the Declaration of Independence

---

4 For a thoughtful analysis of the seeds and fruits of our societal dysfunction, see *Strangers in a Strange Land: Living the Catholic Faith in a Post-Christian World*, Charles J. Chaput, Henry Holt and Co. 2017, particularly chapters 1-7.

and our 2nd President, noted that our government is only meant for a moral and religious people.[5] Laws in and of themselves will not solve the problems we are facing. In fact, it seems that new laws only further isolate factions and increase animosity.[6]

Some people believe that education is the solution. I once had dinner with a couple of my children who are pursuing higher degrees. They were talking about some of the problems we are facing. After discussing the problems from many different angles, the conversation grew a little quiet. Then one of them said, "We're really good at identifying problems, but not so good at finding solutions." In itself, education is not the solution.

There are other people who think that if we just develop and implement the right social programs, that will fix the problems. I have lived through President Johnson's "war on poverty." And there have been program after program after program. Although some poverty has been relieved, it is clear that the true solution evades us. A proponent might argue that we are just not trying the right social program, but I am reminded of one common definition of insanity: doing the same thing over and over again expecting a different result. Social programs alone are not the solution.

And then there is science. Many in the modern world are mesmerized by science. It answers many of our fundamental questions. Through science we have cured many diseases and solved a lot of problems. And modern technology has created all kinds of opportunities for people.

---

5 John Adams, Letter to the Massachusetts Militia, October 11, 1778.
6 See, *The Morality of Consent*, Alexander M. Bickel, Yale University Press, 1977.

But science is merely knowledge (literally, *scientia*). What we do with that knowledge is an entirely different matter. That involves the will, and we have seen the boons of science whittled away by greed and even used for evil purposes. Science, in and of itself, is not the answer.

I grew up in America in the 1960's. I saw the beginnings of the Great Society and the passage of the Civil Rights Act. I saw the rise of Flower Power and heard about the Summer of Love. I saw on the news the tragedy of the Vietnam War and heard a lot of people preaching peace.

But I also remember the assassination of John Kennedy. I remember the days when Bobby Kennedy and then Martin Luther King were shot and killed. I remember the 1968 Democratic convention in Chicago when all of the "peace-niks" turned violent (perhaps in response to Mayor Daley's police tactics, but certainly not Gandhi-esque). I watched as the Civil Rights movement degenerated into armed race conflict between the Ku Klux Klan on one side and the Black Panthers on the other.

All of this suggests that to the extent that people are trying to deal with and fix the mess, none of the "fixes" really work. After years (actually centuries) of trying to solve these problems (and it really has been since the beginning of human history), the mess is still with us.

False Freedom

I don't think that the problem is so much with the solutions. Oftentimes, the proposed solutions have some value. No, I believe that the problem is us. We are too self-absorbed and selfish for any of these solutions to work. Our egos get in the way. We seem to look at the world through the prism of ourselves.

There are people in our society (who I will refer to as secularists) who believe that we alone are sufficient for our own happiness and fulfillment. Every movie, every TV show, every song, every billboard, every magazine article, every blog, everything secularists say and do is about the ultimate goal: it is a search for the complete wholeness of oneself. "Be all that you can be." "Have it your way."

Everything in our society is focused on each person becoming fully self-actualized. According to this philosophy, becoming fully oneself will make a person ultimately happy.[7] But, if our ultimate happiness lies in our becoming fully ourselves, how then do we go about that?

Some believe that in order to achieve this ultimate goal, they must be utterly free from any outside restraints on what they want. And they believe that this kind of freedom is a Right. In the 1992 case of Planned Parenthood v. Casey, Justice Kennedy wrote: "At the heart of liberty is the right to define one's own concept of existence, of meaning, of the universe, and the mystery of human life...."[8]

I must ask, is this correct? Is one free to determine right and wrong for him/herself? Is the fundamental morality of a person's actions simply a matter of his or her individual choice? Are all of our decisions predicated on relativism? The constructs of good and evil, right and wrong, are they up to the vagaries of

---

7 David Brooks in his column "Anthony Kennedy and the Privatization of Meaning" (New York Times, June 28, 2018) argues that modern America has moved from a sense of community to a collection of "monads." He goes on to point out the problems this world view brings with it.

8 Planned Parenthood v. Casey, 505 U.S. 833. ___ (1992)

each single person's definition? Does not a source of morality and ethics govern us all?

What secularists see as freedom, I would call license – license to do anything and everything that we want. In the first century, St. Paul warned us about misunderstanding what freedom really means: true freedom is the freedom to love, not to indulge in fleshly distractions.[9] As Pope St. John Paul II said when he visited the United States in 1995, "[F]reedom consists not in doing what we like, but in doing what we ought."[10]

True freedom is the freedom to love selflessly. The Catechism teaches us that "[t]he more one does what is good, the freer one becomes."[11] It seems that the converse is also true: the more one does what is evil, the less free he or she becomes.

The seculars see any kind of restraint or hindrance on their "freedom," particularly moral or religious, as limiting. In a sense, those limits are a kind of heresy. License – to many, freedom -- is the ultimate rule; any limits that block a person from reaching his or her full potential violate their fundamental belief in freedom.

This secularist understanding of freedom is actually a lie. The belief in this kind of freedom, featuring us at the center, will leave us empty. A casual look at our society shows the bankruptcy of that system of belief: conflict, violence, alienation, tribalism, and all the rest of the things that are plaguing our society.

It is our egocentrism that tries to take God out of the equation. It wants to put the individual at the very center of the universe.

---

9 Gal. 5:13-15

10 Quoted in *Magnificat*, July 2018, Vol. 20, No. 5, page 1.

11 CCC ¶1733. As I discuss later in the section on holiness, sin actually limits our freedom. It binds us. It is like an addictive drug.

But that is an absurd proposition. God is all, and we are nothing but for the love of God. So in a very real sense this faith in a secular freedom leads us to absolutely nothing, to oblivion, to nihilism.

This faith in such a freedom also makes null the entire question of purpose. License does not give any real meaning to our lives. Instead of fulfilling us, it leaves us empty, dissipated. In its most candid moments, even our modern culture knows that this "freedom" - worldly freedom - is unfulfilling. It is not happiness.

So where lies happiness?

Life Seems Meaningless

A life without happiness, without purpose, causes people to despair. In his book *Walden*, Henry David Thoreau (†1862)[12] famously said that, "The mass of men lead lives of quiet desperation." We try to cover up that desperation with lots of noise and bright shiny objects, but in our hearts, we despair.

Some people even see life as meaningless. As Macbeth says,

> *Life is "a tale*
> *told by an idiot,*
> *full of sound and fury.*
> *Signifying nothing."* [13]

We all must recognize that no matter how much success or money we have, or how many things we accumulate, there is always something missing. We feel incomplete. We have a deep-seated dissatisfaction. There is some sort of a deep spiritu-

---

12 Just for clarity, whenever I use the symbol "†" in connection with a date, I am referring to the year when the person died.

13 Macbeth, Act 5, Scene 5.

al longing in us that wants to be satisfied; an emptiness that will never be filled by things.

It is the great malaise: we are unsettled, searching, unsatisfied. We are looking for meaning and purpose to make us happy, and we can't seem to find those things in the world – or in our lives. But to conclude that because we can't find meaning and purpose in our lives, life is meaningless, is a horrible response.

Just because we can't find meaning and purpose doesn't mean they don't exist. It just means that we are looking in the wrong place and not asking the right questions. The way to happiness, it turns out, has been with us always.

God is the Answer

It is not the allurements of the world which make us truly happy. That is because the hole in our hearts, in our souls, is too big for any "thing" in the world to fill. St. Catherine of Siena (†1380) once referred to the world as "poor." What she meant was that there is not enough of anything in the world to fill that spiritual longing in our hearts, at the root of our very being.

St. Catherine of Siena was a lay woman who lived the life of a religious sister in her own home. Through her extensive writings, she exercised great influence over the Popes and bishops of her time. She is recognized as a Doctor of the Church.

More recently, Fr. Reginald Garrigou-Lagrange (†1964) wrote a book entitled *Life Everlasting and the Immensity of the Soul.*[14] In the first section, entitled "Soul Immensity in Our Present Life," he talks about how nothing in this life is big enough to sat-

---

14 Reginald Garrigou-Lagrange, Life Everlasting and the Immensity of the Soul, TAN Books, 1952.

isfy that hunger that all of us have at the center of our being. He wrote, "... our will, although finite, is made to love a good that has no limits."[15] No created thing will fill that vast emptiness at the root of our soul (the wound caused by Original Sin, our separation from God, our ultimate end). Fr. Garrigou-Lagrange goes on to say, "each soul is a universe, *unum versus alia omnia*, because each soul is opened by reason of its intelligence to universal truth, and by its will to universal good."[16]

Similarly, in his "Thanksgiving After Mass," St. Thomas Aquinas describes Heaven as the banquet beyond all telling, where God is the true light, the fullness of all satisfied desires, eternal gladness, consummate delight, and perfect happiness.

That is true happiness, beatitude. The world may give us some temporary pleasure, but it cannot give us that true happiness. That is because the void we are trying to fill is spiritual.

The only thing that can fill that hole is a Person: God. Man is in search of God.[17] It is only Jesus Who is the answer.[18] As St. Augustine († 430) said, God made us for Him, and our hearts are restless until they rest in God.[19]

The Great Commission: Our Challenge

In order to find meaning and purpose in our lives, to be truly happy, we need to turn to God. We need to change our lives, we need to become Christ in the world. Yet, it isn't enough that you and I as random individuals transform our lives and seek clos-

---

15 Ibid. p. 13.
16 Ibid. p. 17.
17 CCC ¶2566.
18 *Guadium et Spes, The Pastoral Constitution on the Church in the Modern World*, Vatican II, ¶¶9-10.
19 "[C]or nostrum inquietum est donec requiescat in Te," *Confessions*, St. Augustine, Book 1, Chapter 1.

er union with God like some eastern religions and philosophies seek to achieve. God's mission, His call, is not just for us alone.

His desire He made clear. "Go therefore and make disciples of all the nations."

Jesus wants everyone to be saved,[20] and we are saved by knowing and loving Him.

What we are called to do in our Christian lives is to work for the conversion of all people. A conversion is "a spiritual change from sinfulness to righteousness...." It is "a change of attitude, emotion, or viewpoint from one of indifference, disbelief, or antagonism to one of acceptance, faith, or enthusiastic support..."[21] As defined in the Catechism, a conversion is a "radical reorientation of the whole life away from sin and evil, and toward God."[22]

We need to ask God to touch the hearts of our loved ones to transform them, to convert them. And it is only through converting those who have not embraced the Word that we will heal the world.

The problem, though, is that secularists want nothing to do with God. They reject the notion of a personal God and the benefits of religion. Those under the spell of secularism more and more view religion as just old-fashioned superstition out of step with our modern understanding and awareness. They claim to be "spiritual," but not religious. Indeed, many see religion itself as the problem. So the question is, what do we do?

The problem is complex: A forced conversion is a lot like forced love – it doesn't exist. The conversion would be purely superficial.

---

20 1 Tim. 2:4
21 https://www.dictionary.com/browse/conversion
22 CCC, Glossary.

Maybe we should just take the time to explain things to our unbelieving friends and family. Our arguments are solid. We have 2,000 years of some of the most brilliant minds that have ever existed who, by the grace of God, have developed the best, most comprehensive arguments ever regarding our faith. Certainly our opponents will see the truth of what we are saying, will they not?

A lot of good Catholics today are heavily into apologetics -- the reasoned explanation of our faith. St. Peter tells us that we should always be ready in charity to give an explanation for our hope and our joy.[23] But that doesn't always work. In fact, I think that explanation rarely works by itself. Having raised 11 children, I know that sometimes we can talk until we are "blue in the face," and people just don't listen. They need to be ready and open to hear what we have to say. So many times, they are not.

St. Paul ran into this problem. Whenever Paul would go to a new town, he would first try to convert the Jews by debating with them in their synagogue. He rarely had any success. He was often beaten, imprisoned, and lashed for his efforts.[24] As was his custom, he then turned to the gentiles. If his message was well received where he was preaching, he would stay to teach those who would listen – sometimes for more than a year.

When he went to Athens, after having failed in the synagogue, he tried to debate with the Athenians in their public squares. The Athenians were intrigued by him, so they took him to the Areopagus, a rugged, stone hill in the lower part of the Acropolis, believed to be the site of the court of Athens, and they asked

---

23 1 Peter: 3:15
24 2 Cor. 11:23-27.

him to tell them all about this "Jesus" and the "Resurrection." The Athenians (like so many Americans today) seemed to be bored and were looking for something new and entertaining.

Paul's speech at the Areopagus[25] was a well-reasoned argument that used certain Greek practices and authors to convince people of the divinity of Jesus.

"The God who made the world and all that is in it, the Lord of Heaven and earth, does not dwell in sanctuaries made by human hands because he needs anything. Rather it is he who gives to everyone life and breath and everything. He made from one the whole human race to dwell on the entire surface of the earth, and he fixed the ordered seasons and the boundaries of their regions, so that people might seek God, even perhaps grope for him and find him, though indeed he is not far from any one of us."

Telling his listeners that they should "seek God, even perhaps grope for him and find him," Paul urged conversion.

Although he did make some converts, St. Paul was discouraged. And so he traveled to Corinth. There, Paul abandoned his rhetorical, philosophical approach. Instead, he focused on the crucifixion, an absurdity to both the Greeks and the Jews. As he says in his first letter to the Corinthians,

"When I came to you, brothers, proclaiming the mystery of God, I did not come with sublimity of words or with wisdom. For I resolved to know nothing while I was with you except Jesus Christ, and him cru-cified. I came to you in weakness and fear and much trembling, and my message and my proclamation were not with persuasive [words of] wisdom, but with a demonstration of spirit and power, so that

---

25 Act 17:22-31

your faith might rest not on human wisdom but on the power of God." [26]

To know nothing except Jesus Christ. That is our goal. That is our mission.

To counter the secularism that besets our country, our families, and our loved ones, and to reform a society immersed in out-of-control destructive behavior, we hold tightly to our faith in God, his message, and his Church, using the weapons he has given us. Conversion calls for a struggle, a battle fought not-so-much with physical weapons or words, as with spiritual weapons.

These weapons are: living a holy life in Christ; seeking to know him through prayer; modeling our own lives on those of the Saints; and sacrificing daily for the souls of our loved ones.

How shall we accomplish this? St. Paul tells us in a letter to the Ephesians:

> *Finally, draw your strength from the Lord and from his mighty power. Put on the armor of God so that you may be able to stand firm against the tactics of the devil. For our struggle is not with flesh and blood but with the principalities, with the powers, with the world rulers of this present darkness, with the evil spirits in the heavens. Therefore, put on the armor of God, that you may be able to resist on the evil day and, having done everything, to hold your ground. So stand fast with your loins girded in **truth**, clothed with **righteousness** as a breastplate, and your feet shod in readiness for **the gospel of peace**. In all circumstances, hold **faith** as a shield, to quench all [the] flaming arrows of the evil one. And take **the helmet of salvation** and **the sword of the Spirit**, which is the word of God.* [27]

---

26 1 Cor. 2:1-5 [Emphasis added.]
27 Eph. 6:10-17. [Emphasis added.]

Such weapons, given to us by God, are enormously powerful.[28] In the face of all of the problems we see in society, in light of the mighty battle we confront to save those we love, we might feel helpless. As weak, puny, and wounded sinners, our spiritual weapons can seem insignificant against the problems of the world: sickness, poverty, cruelty, and fear. We need help.

But in reality, this is not a battle that we fight on our own. In Psalm 33,[29] the psalmist says:

> A king is not saved by a great army,
> nor a warrior delivered by great strength.
> Useless is the horse for safety;
> despite its great strength, it cannot be saved.
> Behold, the eye of the LORD is upon those who fear him,
> upon those who count on his mercy.
> To deliver their soul from death,
> and to keep them alive through famine.[30]

If we turn to and call upon God, He will save us.[31]

The Proposal

What I am proposing here is that we turn to God in prayer, living a life of sacrifice and holiness, and beg Him for help. We need God to touch the hearts of our loved ones; we need Him to save us from the chaos.

In this Handbook, I propose a three-part program of prayer, holiness, and sacrifice. This program involves becoming saints ourselves.

---

28 2 Cor. 10:3-6.
29 See also Psalm 37.
30 Psalm 33:16-19.
31 Joel 2:12-27.

In reading the writings of the Saints and hagiographies (biographies of Saints), one of the consistent messages is that it all begins with *prayer*. In his May 28, 2018, video message to the Pontifical Missions Society, Pope Francis said that "the principal agent of evangelization is the Holy Spirit, and we are called to collaborate with Him." We collaborate with the Holy Spirit through prayer. "Prayer is the first 'missionary work'– the first!" He noted that prayer is the most effective mission work, even if it cannot be measured.[32] So we will begin with prayer.

As St. James tells us, "The fervent prayer of a righteous person is very powerful."[33] Righteousness is acting in accordance with the will of God. I see it as holiness. So to make our prayer effective, we need to practice *holiness*. The second part of the book talks about what that means.

Suffering in this life is not an option; it is just a part of our human condition. The Saints have universally seen the spiritual value of suffering. Jesus told us unless we daily take up our cross and follow Him, we are not fit to be one of His disciples.[34] We take our natural sufferings, offer them to God, and transform them into *sacrifice*. The third section of the book will examine the place of sacrifice in our lives.

As you will see, none of what I say is necessarily new. We as Catholics are not called to innovate. We are just called to pass on the deposit of faith that was given to us by the revelation of Our Lord and Savior, Jesus Christ.

Some may ask why write about this if none of this is new?

The Catholic Church has innumerable practices and tradi-

---

32 National Catholic Register (ncregister.com), Pope Francis: Be Missionaries, Through Prayer, May 28, 2018.

33 James 5:16.

34 Luke 14:27; Matt. 10:38.

tions that shine a sacred light on prayer, holiness, and sacrifice. Yet after Vatican II, the Church adjusted certain aspects of its practices away from traditional expressions of worship in order to emphasize other theological truths. I think there are some traditional practices we need to rediscover. I want to emphasize that this is not a call to return to the pre-Vatican II Church. It is, rather, a call to remember those rituals and those daily habits that will bring us closer to God and allow Him to live in us.

This message is what God through His Son, all of His Saints, and particularly Our Blessed Mother have been telling us. Fr. Andrew Apostoli tells us in *Fatima for Today*, part of the message of Our Lady of Fatima was that we should pray fervently, suffer those misfortunes that God allows to come our way, offer sacrifices to God out of love for Him, and live a holy life.[35]

While not new, in many ways this battle plan is revolutionary. To openly, and maybe even blatantly, live our Catholic faith is totally contrary to what our world, our society, wants us to do. We will be viewed as contrarian, as counter-cultural. We will be treated as odd-balls, outliers, and will be condemned for not conforming to our times. But as St. Paul told us, do not conform to the present age, but be transformed.[36]

So the world is a mess. The solutions the world has to offer do not work. The problems we face are too big for any one of us to fix. God does not want us to be unhappy, but few listen to Him. Since we can't force anyone to accept His solutions or argue them into faith, we can only start with ourselves. We need to develop a close, personal relationship with Him in prayer.

---

35 Fr. Andrew Apostoli, *Fatima for Today*, Ignatius Press 2010, Kindle, Loc. 155.
36 Rom. 12:2.

We need to live our faith to show that we really believe what we say and that what we believe is worth living for. And we need to pray that God will touch the hearts of our families and friends, our communities, our society, our world. If we love selflessly, uncompromisingly, placing God above all things, and through prayer, holiness, and sacrifice offered up for the salvation of our loved ones, our friends, and for the society of man, we can begin to heal our world by bringing others to Christ.

This is our hope, our mission. This is spiritual warfare: spirituality with a purpose.

PART TWO

Prayer

"Rising very early before dawn,
[Jesus] left and went off to a deserted
place, where he prayed." [37]

"The report about him spread all the more,
and great crowds assembled to listen to [Jesus] and to
be cured of their ailments, but he would withdraw
to deserted places to pray." [38]

---

37 Mark 1:35.
38 Luke: 5:15-16.

The first order of discipline in any military outfit is to listen to orders. What good is it to have a military unit consisting of people all doing their own thing? Maybe that is why drill sergeants always seem to be yelling at their new recruits: they need them to focus on what he is saying so that all work in unison. Otherwise, everyone would be doing their own thing, and chaos would reign. It would be like the Tower of Babel.[39] An army where no one listens or follows orders is doomed to be destroyed. Similarly, unless we listen to the guidance of the Holy Spirit (our orders), we will find ourselves unable to pass on the gift of faith. And what the Holy Spirit tells us to do is pray.

In our spiritual life, it is important to understand that prayer is not an option if we want to grow closer to God. It is critical. St. Alphonsus Liguori (†1787) lived in Naples in the 1700's. At that time, the "enlightened" rulers wanted to suppress religious practices and modify them to conform to the times. At first, St. Alphonsus worked in the small towns in the countryside to bring souls to Christ. He was later appointed as the bishop of a small diocese outside of Naples. He believed that, "Those who pray are certainly saved; those who do not pray are certainly damned." [40]

I want to first say something about what prayer is not. In the First Book of Samuel, there is a story of a battle between the Israelites and the Philistines. On the first day of the battle, the Philistines had the better of the fight. That night, the Israelites

---

39 Gen. 11:1-9
40 *Del gran mezzo della preghiera*, quoted at CCC ¶2744.

decided to bring the Ark of the Covenant to the battle front. They thought that with the Ark, they would surely have victory! The next day in battle, the Israelites were defeated and utterly routed.[41]

The reason that God did not save them from defeat was that they were using the

The Ark of the Covenant was the gold covered chest that the Israelites built pursuant to God's instructions. It contained the tablets with the Ten Commandments on them. The Ark symbolized the presence of God among the Israelites.

Ark as some sort of a talisman, a sacred object they could use to control the outcome of events. That is not prayer. Prayer is not magic.

Prayer is a relationship, a relationship with God.[42] But a relationship with God is unlike any of our other relationships. All of our relationships with people are, in a sense, indirect. We don't come into direct contact with another person's soul and experience them in their fullness. We experience other people through our senses: we see them; we hear them; we touch and feel them. We experience our own sensations of the other person, but not them in the totality of their personhood.

With God, it is different. In our relationship with God, He comes into direct contact with our souls. He experiences and knows our very selves. We don't just experience the sensation of God: we experience God Himself. And God, being infinite and all-powerful, His touch can be overwhelming. But that is actually what God wants; He wants us to open up to Him so that He can touch our hearts to make us more like Him.

---

41 1 Samuel 4:1-11.
42 CCC ¶¶2558-65.

It is also important to note that each of us is unique. As a result of that uniqueness, we relate to God in many different ways. Parents pray differently than their children; mothers pray differently than fathers; married individuals pray differently than cloistered nuns and monks. Yet, even with such uniqueness, there are foundational characteristics of prayer that apply to everyone.

I begin this section of the Handbook with reflections on the fundamental aspects of prayer: *simplicity, perseverance,* and *silence.* I call these fundamental because although prayer can (and sometimes does) start under the worst of circumstances, these aspects seem to be necessary for us to develop our prayer lives. Our prayer lives are essential to a relationship with God.

The second part of this section is a survey of different forms of prayer. This survey is admittedly incomplete. It is only intended to provide ideas. Each of us needs, through prayer, to find the best way to pray. It may be the Rosary or some other form of devotional prayer. It may be scripture reading. It may be meditation or contemplation. It may be a combination of all of these. And if one method of prayer gets dry and unrewarding, maybe it is time to try another form. Just keep praying. He is waiting for you. If we knock, He will open.[43] We just need to turn to Him.

And don't be discouraged if God doesn't seem to answer your prayers the way you want Him to. Remember, God is infinite and all powerful. We can ask for Him to do something, but that is all it is: a request. We know that God is all love, so He will al-

---

43 Matt. 7:7; Mark 11:24; Luke 11:9; Rev. 3:20.

ways answer our prayers, but also since He is all love, He may not answer our prayers in the way that we want. He will do what is best for us.

Fundamentals of Prayer

Prayer Takes Time.

In the first letter of John, the Beloved Apostle tells us that anyone who does not love does not know God, because "God is love."[44] He doesn't say that God loves us (which He certainly does), but rather that the very essence of God is love.

When some theologians and Saints talk about the Trinity, they say that the Word (Jesus) was begotten by God the Father out of love, and that the love between the Father and the Son is so powerful, that love itself is a Divine Person, the Holy Spirit. The love that exists within the Holy Trinity is fundamental and profound. To repeat, God is love.

Since God is love, it seems appropriate that what God wants from us most is that we love Him, and all of His creation is a reflection of Him. That is why when the Pharisee asked Jesus "Teacher, which commandment in the law is the greatest?" [45] Jesus said, "You shall love the LORD, your God, with all your heart, with all your soul, and with all your mind." [46] And then Jesus volunteered the second commandment: "You shall love your neighbor as yourself." [47] God is all about love.

Love is a funny thing, though. We can't really love what we

---

44 1 John 4:8.

45 Matthew 22:36

46 Matt. 22:37.

47 Matt. 22:39.

don't know. That love would be very abstract, almost unreal. In order to truly love someone, we have to know him or her. And if we really do love someone, we *have* a strong desire or even a need to know them.

God calls us to love Him. In order to love God, we need to know Him. And that takes time. The time we spend in prayer allows us to move closer to God, to know Him.

The Psalmist says, "Be still and know that I am God."[48] The only way to get to know God is to spend time with Him. Spending time with him means getting away from all of the distractions in our lives - the TV, the radio, the computer, our phones, or other devices. If we really want to love God, we need on a regular basis (daily) to set aside quiet time to get to know Him through prayer.

St. Francis de Sales (†1622) was the bishop of Geneva, a diocese that at the time was almost completely Calvinist. He was prohibited from preaching and saying Mass in his own diocese, but he persevered by printing leaflets on the relatively new invention of the printing press and under the cover of night, slipping them under the doors of the citizens of his diocese. He notably said that every Christian should spend 30 minutes a day in prayer, unless they were busy – and then they need an hour.

Christianity is not just a set of rules about how to live our lives and be happy. It is not just a philosophy. Christianity is fundamentally a relationship with a Person, Jesus Christ, and prayer is *the* foundation of that relationship. And that takes time.

Be Silent

So prayer takes time, but what are we doing in prayer? What "happens"?

---

48 Psalm 46:11.

After Elijah destroyed the prophets of Baal,[49] Jezebel, the evil queen of Israel, sought his life. Elijah fled to Mt. Horeb. Mt. Horeb was the same mountain where God appeared to Moses and revealed His Name. When Elijah got to Mt. Horeb, he hid in a cave. God called him out of the cave and said that He would pass by.

As Elijah waited, a strong wind came, so strong that it was "rending the mountains and crushing rocks before the LORD." But God was not in the wind.

Next came an earthquake that shook the mountain. But God was not in the earthquake.

After the earthquake, fire swept across the mountain. But again, God was not in the fire.

But after the fire, Elijah heard a still, small voice, a whisper. And when he heard that, Elijah hid his face. He knew that God was in that whisper.[50]

In my prayer, I experience God as a quiet Presence. I feel Him more than anything. It is a very subtle thing, but also very powerful. It seems to originate from outside of me ... more probably from deep within me.

We can easily drown out that still, small voice, that Presence. Modern society does all that it can to distract us from it with TVs, radios, cell phones, iPads, magazines, billboards, and all other kinds of noise and distractions. If we want to come to know God, we need to silence all of these distractions and listen for

---

49   See 1 Kings 18, a great story by the way.
50   1 Kings 19:1-13.

that still, quiet voice.[51] Attentiveness of the heart is essential to prayer.[52] Contemplative prayer is silence.[53]

St. Faustina Kowalska (†1938) was a Polish nun and mystic. She grew up in a large and poor but devout family. When she was 19, while at a dance with her sister, she had a vision of Christ calling her to her vocation. After some setbacks and delays, she entered the Congregation of Our Lady of Mercy on August 1, 1925. In April of 1927, she entered a very dark period in her spiritual life where she felt abandoned by God. This is not uncommon for mystics. This lasted for about a year. Otherwise, Sr. Faustina led an ordinary life working in the convent bakery and the kitchen. But on February 22, 1931, she had another vision of Jesus, the image of Divine Mercy which has spread throughout the entire world. She died in 1938 a year before the Nazis invaded Poland. She once said, "Silence is so powerful a language that it reaches the throne of the living God."[54]

What we listen to, look at, or spend time with affects us. We may not notice it, or if we do, we may deny it. Nonetheless, the noise around us affects us. Listen to the words of the songs that people sing all the time. Think about what it is that is on TV. From a Christian perspective, it is all pretty disturbing. If we are constantly bombarded (and we voluntarily subject ourselves to all of this) with those kinds of messages, I think that we will become acclimated to those messages. They will all seem to be so normal, and they're not. They are a grotesque perversion of re-

---

51 For a compelling reflection on the need for silence in our prayer life, see *The Power of Silence*, by Cardinal Sarah, Ignatius Press (2017)

52 CCC ¶2570.

53 CCC ¶2717.

54 *Divine Mercy in My Soul, Diary of Saint Maria Faustina Kowalska*, ¶ 888. 6287, Marian Press (2914)

ality. We need to shut out all of that cacophony, and listen to the voice of God that quietly whispers the truth in our hearts.

The need for silence is appropriate, given who God is. God is the infinity of all infinities and the perfection of all perfections. Many times in the Old Testament we are told that if anyone saw God, he or she would be overwhelmed and die.[55] Yet God does not want to overwhelm us; he wants us to love Him. So in order to give us the freedom to love Him, He comes to us in a still, small whisper. Listen for it.

> *"But the LORD is in his holy temple;*
> *silence before him, all the earth."* [56]

Prayer Can Be Simple

St. Jean Vianney (†1859) is the patron Saint of pastors. He grew up during the French Revolution when being a Catholic was a capital offense punishable by death. When old enough, he was drafted by Napoleon's army to fight the Spanish. He was so sick that he fell behind in the marching. If he had been caught, he would have been shot for desertion, but instead, he was found by a rebel who took him high up into the mountains to hide. Vianney couldn't come out until Napoleon was gone. Because of that, his education was very spotty.

While he was in the mountains, he discerned his vocation to be a priest. But because of his poor education, he flunked out of the seminary his first year. All of his classes and homework and tests were in Latin, which he had not learned and could not speak. His parish priest took him under his wing and tutored him so that he could be readmitted to the seminary. He barely

---

55 Ex. 33:20; 20:19; Numbers 3:10; 3:38; and Judges 13:22.
56 Habakkuk 2:20.

graduated and eventually was sent to a remote parish in the little town of Ars (maybe 200 families) where religion was the last thing on the villagers' minds.

Fr. Vianney turned the town around. Within a few years, the citizens were all going to Mass. People from all over France and beyond would go to Ars to go to confession with Fr. Vianney. He regularly would fight (both physically and spiritually) with the devil at night. He also fasted and prayed constantly. Numerous miracles were attributed to him even during his lifetime. He was clearly a Saint.[57]

There is a story that after saying Mass, he would walk through the church to go to the confessional. He began to notice an old, retired farmer who would sit in church after Mass just staring at the crucifix. One day, Fr. Vianney stopped and asked the old farmer what he was doing. The old farmer looked at Fr. Vianney and said, "Well, sometimes I look at Him, and sometimes He looks at me." [58]

Sometimes prayer can be that simple. Silent. Contemplative. Intimate.

Prayer is Work

I once read a story about St. Bernard of Clairvaux (†1153). (Whether it is true or not, I don't know, but it makes a good point.) St. Bernard was born into a noble family, but he decided to enter a Cistercian monastery at 23. The Cistercians, also known as the Trappists, are a Benedictine religious order of monks and nuns dedicated to prayer, living primarily in silence. When he entered, he brought with him his brothers, cousins,

57 Francois Trochu, *The Cure D'Ars: St. Jean-Marie-Baptiste Vianney*, Tan Books (2009).
58 cf. CCC ¶2715.

friends, and eventually even his father. There were 30 new monks in all. He founded a new monastery and became its abbot. All he wanted was to be a simple monk, but he soon was called on to settle political disputes and reconcile church factions throughout Europe.

One time when he was traveling to a meeting between two rival factions, he was riding a horse. He

The Benedictines, and the various orders that grew out of them, were founded by St. Benedict (†547). Generally they are monastic communities that take vows of poverty, chastity, and obedience to the abbot or abbess. The motto of the Benedictines is "Ora et labora" ("Prayer and work"). I think it is fair to say that it was the Benedictines and related monastic communities that preserved Western culture after the fall of the Roman empire.

passed a peasant working by the road. The peasant looked up and grunted. St. Bernard stopped and asked what was wrong. The peasant said, "Look at you riding that big horse while I'm down here breaking my back working. All you ever have to do is pray all day."

St. Bernard reportedly objected by saying, "Prayer isn't easy, you know." The peasant scoffed again, so St. Bernard extended an offer to him. If the man could say one Our Father all the way through without getting distracted and staying focused, St. Bernard would give him his horse.

The peasant began: "Our Father, Who art in heaven, hallowed be Thy... Wait, does the saddle come with it?"

St. Bernard kept his horse.

Prayer shouldn't be just a casual rattling off of rote prayers. Prayer should be a concentrated effort to focus on God, to listen to that still, small voice. We must strive to keep out our distractions, although they will come nonetheless. And we have to be honest with ourselves – brutally honest. Are we praying for our own benefit only out of self-love, or are we sincerely and humbly reaching out to God, stripping ourselves of all of our personal idols, all those things in our lives that get between us and God? To grow close to God in prayer, it takes patience, discipline, and real effort. Prayer is work.

Prayer Must Be Constant

Prayer needs to be constant. If we pray for a little while and then stop for a little while, we get nowhere. If we are not moving forward, we may think we are standing still, but we are actually backsliding in our spiritual life.

This need for constancy can be illustrated by a story about Moses. At one time, while leading the Israelites through the desert, the Amalekites, an ancient tribal enemy of Israel, attacked. While the Israelite army fought on the plain, Moses went up a mountain with Aaron and Hur. Moses initially raised his hands (in prayer), and the Israelites had the better of the fight. However, Moses grew tired and lowered his hands. When he did, the Amalekites had the better of the fight. So Aaron and Hur had Moses sit on a rock, and they held up his arms. "And Joshua defeated Amelek and his people with the sword." [59]

What this story illustrates is that as long as we continue to pray, God will support us in our efforts; He will fight for us. When we don't ask for God's help, He won't force it on us. He is more than willing to come to our aid, but we need to continuously ask for

---

[59] Ex. 17: 8-16.

His help. As the Catechism points out, "it is necessary to pray always without ceasing and with the *patience* of faith." [60]

Brother Lawrence of the Resurrection (†1691) is another good example. We don't know much about him personally. He was born Nicholas Herman in what is now a part of eastern France. He grew up very poor. When he was old enough, he joined the army which provided him with regular meals and a place to sleep. It appears that as a soldier he lived a pretty dissolute life. Following an injury, he left the army and worked as a servant for a while.

Eventually, Nicholas decided to join the Discalced Carmelites. The Discalced (i.e., shoeless) Carmelites are a reform of the Carmelite Order that was originally founded in the 12th century on Mt. Carmel in present-day Israel. It was founded by former Crusaders who wanted to dedicate their lives to prayer. When the Muslims invaded, the Carmelites were forced out of the Holy Land. Over time in Europe, many of their ascetic practices lapsed. According to some reports, they gave up on silence; they gave up on poverty; they gave up on seclusion; they gave up on fasting; they gave up on prayer. They became a comfortable social club.

In the 1500's, Sts. Teresa (†1582) and John of the Cross (†1591) (originally members of the Carmelite Order) were inspired to form the Discalced Carmelites and return to the more primitive observance of their Rule with poverty (hence the "shoeless"), fasting, silence, seclusion, and prayer being the central focus of the new order. And the Order has produced some exception-

---

60 CCC ¶2613.

al Saints, including Sts. Theresa of Lisieux (†1897) and Theresa Benedicta of the Cross (†1942).

Nicholas applied to the Discalced Carmelite priory in Paris and was accepted. It was there that he took the name Brother Lawrence of the Resurrection. He had no formal education, so he joined as a lay brother. He had dreams of spending long hours in prayer and contemplation, but he was assigned to the kitchen. It was a large priory, and there was a lot of food to prepare and serve, and a lot of dishes to gather and clean. It was not what he had thought he was getting into when he signed up.

Over time, however, Br. Lawrence came to realize that God doesn't need the beauty of a basilica or the quiet of a cloister to touch your heart. We do not need an exalted place to pray. We only need to pray and to pray often. He realized that wherever God puts us, that's where He wants us to be. And when he puts us somewhere, it is for some reason – and He doesn't forget us. Nor should we forget Him or our relationship with Him. Ever.

People began to notice the deep peace that exuded from Br. Lawrence even in the midst of the chaos of the kitchen. They began to seek his counsel and advice. People would write him letters asking for guidance which he would freely give.

Br. Lawrence died in relative obscurity. However, the letters that he had sent to various people in Paris circulated among the faithful. So many people were inspired by these letters that the vicar general of the Archdiocese of Paris compiled Br. Lawrence's writings and the recollections of his Prior into a book that we now know as *The Practice of the Presence of God.*[61] Although Br. Lawrence struggled with prayer early, he came to realize

---

61 Brother Lawrence of the Resurrection, *The Practice of the Presence of God*, Image Books/Doubleday (1977), © 1977 by John J. Delaney.

that "prayer was simply an awareness of the presence of God ..." [62] at all times and under all circumstances. Whether working in the kitchen or in the shoe repair shop, he was "glad to do any task, however small, for the love of God." [63] Although he said "we should establish ourselves in the presence of God by continually talking to Him," [64] "he was gratified when he could pick up a straw from the ground for the love of God, seeking Him alone and nothing else, not even His gifts." [65] Br. Lawrence felt that the constancy of prayer was imperative, and "it was a shameful thing to allow thoughts of trivial things to break into this conversation [with God]." [66]

It cannot be emphasized enough that prayer is not a numbers game. Jesus condemned that. [67] The distinction is that prayer, above all, is about a relationship. God wants to have a personal relationship with each and every one of us. And spotty, on-again, off-again relationships are shallow. Prayer must be constant, especially amid the clamor of our contemporary society.

Prayer Specifics

Now I want to move into some prayer specifics. These are some of the more common forms of prayer. But although they are common, they are nonetheless valuable.

The Jesus Prayer

In the Gospel of Luke, Jesus told a parable about a Pharisee and

---

62 Ibid. p. 38.
63 Ibid p. 29.
64 Ibid p. 24.
65 Ibid p. 26.
66 Ibid p. 24.
67 Matt. 6:7.

a tax collector who went up to the temple to pray. [68] The Pharisee thanked God that he was so righteous and not like other men such as the tax collector. He then listed all of the "holy" things that he did, in effect bragging to God.

The tax collector, on the other hand, stood in the back of the temple. He did not even lift his eyes up to Heaven. Instead, he beat his breast in sorrow and said, "God, be merciful to me a sinner."

Jesus pointed out that it was the tax collector's prayer that was heard, not the Pharisee's. He said, "Whoever exalts himself will be humbled; but whoever humbles himself will be exalted." [69] As pointed out in the Catechism, humility is the foundation of prayer. [70]

A life of prayer has called to Christians throughout the ages. During the persecution of the Christians by the Romans, some Christians hid in the desert, living out their Christian lives, lives of solitary reflection. But after the Emperor Constantine issued the Edict of Milan in 313 A.D. which permitted Christianity in the Roman Empire, there was a second wave of Christians going to the desert for a different reason. Since the emperor appeared to favor Christianity, it became somewhat fashionable to be a Christian. Some saw this as a softening of the Christian discipline; those Christians seeking a more rigorous relationship with Christ also fled to the desert. This was the beginning of the desert solitaries ("monachoi" in Greek, monks in English) who gathered together into communities which grew into monasteries.

---

68 Luke 18:9-14.
69 Matthew 23:12; but see also Luke 14:4
70 CCC ¶2559.

Deep in the arid desert, alone, bereft of civilization, the monks looked for ways to pray. They, of course, knew the Gospel stories. Recalling the parable of the Pharisee and the tax collector, over time, they developed what has come to be known in one form or another as the *Jesus Prayer*:

> *Lord Jesus Christ, Son of the Living God,*
> *have mercy on me, a sinner.*

In this simple prayer, we acknowledge Jesus as our Lord and the son of God; we acknowledge our status as sinners; and we ask for God's mercy. By invoking the name of Jesus, which means "Yahweh saves," we invite Him into our hearts to animate and transfigure our lives. [71] The monks made a habit of praying the Jesus Prayer throughout the day.

Although Jesus told us not to multiply our words in prayer, [72] He did tell His disciples to pray always.[73] So the "Jesus Prayer" is a simple prayer that we can pray throughout the day. We can pray it when we get up. We can grab a moment at a stoplight and pray it. While waiting for an elevator, we can pray it. We can pray it when we enter a church. Prayerfully repeating it over and over reflecting on what we are saying is a beautiful way to meditate on our relationship with God.

Praying this simple prayer throughout the day can help us, maybe just for that brief moment, to focus on Jesus, recalling that He is God, and that He is all merciful. Like I mentioned earlier, prayer doesn't have to be complicated; it can be simple. And Jesus promises that this prayer will be heard.

---

71 CCC ¶¶2666-2669.
72 Matthew 6:7.
73 Luke 18:1.

The Our Father

In the Gospels, we read that Jesus often went off alone to pray. [74] It may seem odd that the Son of God would go to pray. He is the Second Person of the Holy Trinity, so why would Jesus need to go pray? We must remember that although Jesus was fully God, He was also fully man. And as a man, He had to pray. I believe that He also wanted to be an example for us.

When the Apostles asked Jesus, "Lord, teach us to pray," [75] He gave them the Our Father. If we look at this prayer, it, too, is really a very short, simple prayer. We often rattle it off without even thinking. It consists of seven petitions that can be divided into two sections: the first three petitions focus on the love of God; and the remaining four petitions focus on love of neighbor. This is consistent with the two greatest commandments: love God and love your neighbor. [76] We pray this prayer all the time, but it is good to take some time to think about each one of these petition.

"Hallowed be Thy Name" [77] – in this petition, we honor God's name. God is the pure essence of holiness. That is what hallowed means: to be made holy. He is Holy beyond anything you and I could ever imagine. During Jesus' time, and even to this day, most Jews feel it is a sacrilege even to utter the name of God. There's nothing we can do to add to the holiness of God's name. But we can detract from it. If we call ourselves Catholic or even Christian and live in a secular way, conforming to society around us without regard to the teachings of Christ, we dishonor the Name of Christ. By our sins, we decrease the holiness of

---

74 Matt. 14:23; Mark 1:35; Luke 5:16 and 6:12.
75 Luke 11:1.
76 Matt. 22:36-40.
77 CCC ¶¶ 2807-2815.

God's name in us and for others. So to me, this petition is a call to holiness for us. It is a call to live our faith and give glory to God.

"Thy Kingdom come" [78] – in this petition, we pray for the coming of the Kingdom of God in our time. The Kingdom of God is both spiritual and physical. On the spiritual level, it is a communion with God that results in the "peace that is beyond understanding." [79] On the physical level, in the Gospel of Matthew, when Jesus prophesizes about the last judgment and the separation of the sheep from the goats, He tells us, the kingdom of God is caring for the poor, the sick, the widows, and orphans. [80] But the coming of the Kingdom has an eschatological dimension as well: the Kingdom will come at the end of time. So this petition is also a prayer for the Second Coming.

"Thy Will be done on earth as it is in heaven" [81] – God is all-powerful. In the end, nothing will frustrate His Will. He will blend the dissonance of sin into the beautiful symphony of creation. But we are called to cooperate in the "plan" of God. Sin is a substitution of our personal will over the Will of God. We must submit to His Will, and we must do so with grace and boundless gratitude.

When Gabriel appeared to Mary and asked her to be the Mother of God, the universe held its breath waiting for her answer. She said, "May it be done to me according to your word," [82] and the universe shouted with joy. When Jesus was in the Garden of Gethsemane, He prayed, "Father... not my will but yours be done." [83] Jesus and Mary, the two greatest examples of submis-

---

78 CCC ¶¶ 2816-2821.
79 Philippians 4:7.
80 Matt. 25:31-46.
81 CCC ¶¶ 2822-2827.
82 Luke 1:38.
83 Luke 22:42.

sion to the will of God for our own lives, humbly submitted their wills to the Will of God in their own lives, and so should we. [84] And it is in His will that we find our peace.[85]

"Give us this day our daily bread" [86] – this petition marks a shift in the prayer. The first three petitions focus on God, and now we turn to our own needs. As developed in the Catechism, this petition has several levels. First, it is a recognition of our dependence on God for all of our basic needs. We are asking God to provide us with sustenance.[87] In addition, as the Catechism points out, the presence in our world of those who are hungry or even starving demands that those who have a surplus must share with those who are in need.[88] Finally, the Greek work (*epiousios*) that St. Jerome translated as "daily" (*quotidianum*) appears nowhere else in the Bible (or anywhere else in Greek literature, I have been told). Literally it means "super-substantial," or as the Catechism puts it, "super-essential." It is clearly a reference to the Eucharist, the Bread of Life, the Body of Christ. So this petition is a petition that God supply us with our necessities in life, a call to us to share with those in the world who are in need, and a prayer for the Eucharist.

"And forgive us our trespasses, as we forgive those who trespass against us" [89] – this is the only petition that has a condition attached to it. We are asking that our sins be forgiven but only to the extent that we forgive the sins of others. And Jesus tells us we must never stop forgiving the sins of others.[90]

---

84 1 Samuel 15:22, obedience is better than sacrifice
85 Albegheri Dante, *Paradiso* – Canto III, line 85.
86 CCC ¶¶ 2828-2837
87 CCC ¶¶ 2828-2830.
88 CCC ¶ 2831.
89 CCC ¶¶ 2838-2845.
90 See Matt. 18:21-35.

"Lead us not into temptation" [91] – It cannot be emphasized enough that God does not lead us into temptation. He helps us to avoid it.[92] He wants to set us free from the slavery to sin. The Catechism explains that it is difficult to translate the Greek verb used here into a single English word. It means both "do not allow us to enter into temptation" and "do not let us yield to temptation." Cornelius à Lapide (†1637), in his *Great Biblical Commentary*, explained it like this: "Permit us not to be led into temptation in such a manner, at least, that we are overcome by it, as fishes and birds are taken in a net." This petition is a request that we be delivered from our own sinful tendencies. Protect us from temptation, Lord.

"And deliver us from evil" [93] – The Catechism says this is personal - "deliver us from the evil one." It is reminiscent of our baptismal promises. This is a request that we be protected from Satan, and all his works, and all his empty promises.

The first reason why we should take the time to prayerfully reflect on this prayer is that when the Apostles asked Jesus to teach them to pray, this is how He answered them. Our Lord and Savior, Jesus Christ, the Second Person of the Blessed Trinity, the Word through Whom all things were made, told us to pray in this way. We would be foolish to pass over it lightly.

In addition, the Saints have admonished us to pray the Our Father. Although it is a very simple prayer, St. Thomas Aquinas described it as perfect and wrote extensively about it.[94] He wrote that "[a]mong all other prayers, the Lord's Prayer holds the chief

---

91 CCC ¶¶ 2846-2849.
92 James 1:13.
93 CCC ¶¶ 2850-2854.
94 Summa Theologiae, Secunda Secundae Partis, Question 83, Article 9 for example.

place. It has five excellent qualities which are required in all prayer. A prayer must be confident, ordered, suitable, devout and humble." [95] St. Augustine commented in some detail on the Our Father in his Letter to Proba, a wealthy Roman widow who with many other women had sought refuge in Carthage, North Africa, after the sack and pillage of Rome in 410. He told her:

"For whatever words we may say – whether the desire of the person praying go before the words, and employ them in order to give definite form to its requests, or come after them, and concentrate attention upon them, that it may increase in fervor – if we pray rightly, and as becomes our wants, we say nothing but what is already contained in the Lord's prayer. And whoever says in prayer anything which cannot find its place in that gospel prayer, is praying in a way which, if it be not unlawful, is at least not spiritual...." [96]

Many other Saints have also reflected deeply on the Our Father. One of the most famous reflections, perhaps, is included in a book entitled *The Way of Perfection* by St. Teresa of Avila. [97] In it, Teresa talks about prayer generally, but in particular she focuses on the Our Father which was her favorite prayer:

"Consider the words uttered by the Divine lips: the very first of them will show you at once what love He has for you, and it is no small blessing and joy to see that [He] loves [you]." [98]

The question for us, though, is how many of us have really taken the time to think about what we are praying when we pray

95 Thomas Aquinas, *The Catechetical Instructions*, translated by Joseph B. Collins, Veritatis Splendor Publications (2012).

96 New Advent, Church Fathers: Letter 130 (St. Augustine), http://www.newadvent.org/fathers/1102130.htm.

97 See also, St. Cyprian, *Treatise on the Lord's Prayer*.

98 St. Teresa of Avila, *The Way of Perfection*, translated and edited by E. Allison Peers, Ignacio Hills Press (2009, 1st Ed.)

the Our Father. We (me included) typically pray it without thinking about it. That has some value to it, but not the full value. We get more from the prayer (any prayer, really) by slowing down and reflecting on it as we pray. Why did Jesus tell us to pray this prayer? Why these petitions in particular? And what do they mean to you and me here today?

Since this is the prayer that Jesus gave us to pray, I think regularly taking a little time to think about each of the petitions would be worthwhile. Although the Our Father is short enough to pray while waiting in a line at the grocery store, it is also a good prayer to pray in those quiet moments when we can reflect on what each petition means to us in particular.

The Psalms

As I mentioned earlier, Jesus prayed. Throughout His ministry, He would pray. He would get up early in the morning and go pray.[99] He prayed before major events such as the miracles of the loaves and the raising of the dead.[100] He prayed all night before choosing the apostles.[101] In addition, Jesus thought that prayer was so important that He took the time to teach his disciples how to pray, and He gave us the Our Father.

But what did Jesus *pray*? The only thing that the Gospels say is that Jesus went off alone to pray, but it doesn't tell us anything more. The Catechism tells us that Jesus' prayer before major events was a humble and trusting submission of His human will to the loving will of His Father.[102] I am sure that He was in deep contemplative prayer being fully human. Since He is also divine,

---

99 Mark 1:35, Luke 5:16.
100 Mark 6:32, John 11:41-42.
101 Luke 6:12-13.
102 CCC ¶2600.

I don't know how accessible that would be to us. But I think there is another possibility.

When Jesus was hanging on the Cross, He cried out, "My God, My God, why have You forsaken me?"[103] That troubled me for a long time. How could God the Father have forsaken His Son, Jesus, with whom he was united in his very substance? That made no sense to me. Our God is One and Three, but He is still One. How could the Son be separated from the Father? So I wondered why Jesus would have said that.

But if we look at the footnote for that verse, it refers us back to Psalm 22. Psalm 22 starts off with those very words:

> *"My God, my God, why have you abandoned me?*
> *Why so far from my cry for help,*
> *from my cries of anguish?"* [104]

This Psalm starts off with a lamentation of the Psalmist's rejection by God and by man. The middle part of the Psalm is a prayer for deliverance. The end of the Psalm is a song of thanksgiving and victory. So in a way, Psalm 22 is a prayer of hope during a crisis.[105]

That was when it dawned on me that Jesus would have prayed the Psalms (the "Praises").[106] They were the liturgical prayers of the Jewish communities - Jesus' community - when they gathered at the synagogues. Although the Psalms are traditionally attributed to King David (circa 1000 BC), most scholars agree that they were written over an extended period of time. Some, such as Psalm 22, seem to date back to the reign of King David,

---

103 Matthew 27:46.
104 Psalm 22:2.
105 When Jesus said, "Father, into your hands, I commend my spirit," he was also quoting from Psalm 31:6.
106 CCC ¶2586.

but others clearly refer to the Babylonian Captivity (587-538 BC, although historians disagree on how to date this precisely). Over time, these prayers were collected into scrolls, copied, and distributed to the various synagogues. These were the prayers that Jesus would have prayed in the synagogues and at the Temple.

The Psalms were written for almost every conceivable need or desire. There are Psalms that are like a cry from the depths of our souls. There are Psalms that celebrate the loving trust in God. There are Psalms of repentance. There are Psalms in time of need. There are Psalms of thanksgiving. There are Psalms of praise. There are Psalms expressing our desire for God.

As a Jew, Jesus would have prayed the Psalms, and I believe that He was praying the 22nd Psalm while

A Cry for Help
Psalm 130
Out of the depths I
call to you, Lord;
LORD, hear my cry.

A Prayer of Trust
Psalm 23
The Lord is my shepherd;
There is nothing I lack.

Trust in God
Psalm 27
The Lord is my light
and my salvation;
Whom do I fear?
The Lord is my life's refuge:
Of whom am I afraid.

The Prayer of A Sinner
Psalm 51
Have mercy on me, God,
in your kindness.
In your compassion
blot out my offense.

He hung on the Cross. Yes, He was praying the Psalm, but He was simultaneously living in that moment. Being the Word of God, many of the Psalms are His actual words. In fact, the early Church Fathers noted that in praying the Psalms, Jesus made them His own. In a sense, He "Christified" (my word) them.[107]

The desert monks who had fled society in the 3rd and 4th centuries AD to lead a monastic life took to heart St. Paul's advice to pray always.[108] Focusing exclusively on God through fasting and prayer, many of them would pray all 150 Psalms each day. Since that interfered with things like farming and cooking, that practice was relaxed to praying them on a weekly basis. This custom of praying all of the Psalms on a regular basis spread throughout the Church and today is what has come to be known as the Divine Office or the Liturgy of the Hours, which consist of seven times of prayer daily.

But how should we pray the Psalms? Slowly, thoughtfully, of course. Think about who

In Time of Need
Psalm 86
Hear me, Lord, and answer me,
For I am poor and oppressed.
Preserve my life, for I am loyal;
Save your servant
who trusts in you.

Thanks to God
Psalm 145
All your works give you
thanks, O Lord,
And your faithful bless you.
They speak of the glory
of your reign
And tell of your great works.

In Praise of God
Psalm 100
Shout joyfully to the
Lord, all you lands;
Worship the Lord with
cries of gladness;
Come before him with
joyful song.

A Prayer of Longing
Psalm 42
As the deer longs for running
water,
So my soul longs for you,
O God.

---

107 For a beautiful reflection on the Psalms as prayer, see St. Ambrose, *Explanation of the Psalms*, Liturgy of the Hours, Office of Readings, Tenth Week, Friday and Saturday; see also Pope St. Pius X, apostolic constitution Divino afflatu, introduction.

108 1 Thess. 5:17; Romans 12:12.

is speaking in the Psalm. Sometimes we can clearly hear the voice of Jesus. Other times, it is a poor soul suffering terrible pain or persecution and asking for God's help and protection. The Psalm may be one of rejoicing over a gift the pray-er has received. At other times it may be someone rejoicing over the beauty of God's creation and the many blessings God has given to us. It is interesting to notice how many times a Psalm is about a military engagement, which I understand to be our spiritual battle. We read a lot about Jerusalem or the Temple which I interpret as the Church. In all of the Psalms, we should consider how the Psalm mirrors our own life in some way. How did Christ's life, death, and resurrection mirror that prayer? We need to make the Psalms our own prayers just like Christ made them His own.

As Catholics, we are told to pray without ceasing. Praying the Divine Office (or maybe just parts of it) is a good way to achieve that. There is a 4 volume set available, but the Office is also available on our smart phones; a good use of technology. We can listen to the Office and pray it on the way to and from work. An abbreviated version called Christian Prayer is also available. I realize that people's lives are busy, so maybe just taking the time to pray a Psalm or two a day is all we can fit in, but even then, we are praying with Jesus.

Lectio Divina

Lectio divina is a tradition in which monks and contemplative nuns did not so much look at the Bible as something simply to be studied (which, of course, it can be), but rather as something to be read, meditated on, lived, and loved. It is a way of approaching the Bible as the Word of God made real to us each and every day.

When St. Augustine was in Milan at the time of his conversion, he heard someone say, "Tolle, lege," or in English, "Take, read." He went to his room, opened his Bible, and read, "...it is the hour now for you to awake from sleep .... [P]ut on the Lord Jesus Christ, and make no provision for the desires of the flesh." [109] He read and then did as the divine revelation commanded him. And he never turned back.

Early in his ministry, St. Francis of Assisi (†1226) asked a priest to randomly open the Gospels three times and read the first verses that he saw. They were Matthew 19:21, Luke 9:3, and Matthew 16:24, telling him to sell what he had, give everything to the poor, and follow Jesus. And that's what he did ... for the rest of his life.

Many Saints have had similar experiences where God has spoken to them through the Bible.

The Bible is not a dead book. It is the living Word of God. God speaks to us through the Bible, but always in connection with the Tradition of the Church of which the Bible itself is a product. That is why at every Mass, every day, throughout the world, sections of the Bible are read, and the priest or deacon explains how we should apply those verses to our daily lives.

God speaks to us in private as well, such as what happened to St. Augustine and St. Francis. God speaks to us through His Word. He will console us during times of trial or suffering; He will help us see what He is calling us to do; He will fill us with joy for no reason whatsoever. But He also speaks to us through the Bible.

---

109 Rom. 13:11 and 13:14.

Our world is full of useless (and even destructive) noise. It is difficult to quiet our mind. I heard one person say that with everything going on in her life, her mind is like a tree full of monkeys. I like that image.

But God speaks to us in a still, quiet voice. To hear what God is saying to us in the Bible, we need to go to a quiet place, still our minds from all our worldly cares and distractions, and slowly read a short section of the Bible. What section we choose doesn't really matter; just trust in God, and listen in your heart. Something will certainly pop out as if the Holy Spirit were using a highlighter. Stop reading more, and just read that section, that sentence, that phrase, or maybe even just that word … over and over. See what it is that God is trying to say to you.

Lectio divina can also involve reading what the Saints have written about various passages in the Bible. There are resources available to us online (the USCCB sometimes will send things out, as well as FlockNotes). One of those is the *Catena Aurea* (the "Golden Chain") by Thomas Aquinas, which is a collection of biblical commentary by the Church Fathers that was collected by St. Thomas. These resources can be very helpful, but they are not necessary.

Although *lectio divina* can take almost any form of quiet, slow, thoughtful reading of the Bible, there is a traditional understanding of it. According to that tradition, there are four "moments" in *lectio divina*. The first (after quieting our hearts and minds – to the extent possible) is reading, or *leggere*. This is not speed reading. This is picking out a short passage of scripture and reading it slowly, thoughtfully, listening to what God is saying in that passage. Let it sink in.

The second moment is meditation, or *meditare*. In reading, something will jump out. Chew on that. Turn it over in your mind. See what it is that God is trying to say in that sentence, phrase, word, or idea. Take time with this.

The third moment is prayer, or *pregare*. This is where you talk to God about what that thing He brought to your attention means to you right where you are that very day.

The final moment is contemplation, or *contemplare*. This is described as the point where we leave thinking (and talking) behind and just allow our hearts to speak to or commune with God. To me, this is the most difficult because of all the monkeys. I have a hard time just being with God without things popping into my head. All of the spiritual advisers I have read say to be patient. Don't be discouraged. Wait for God to reach out. He certainly will. He wants this more than we do.

Although *lectio divina* began as a prayer method for members of contemplative religious orders, it is not limited to them. All of us can (and should) take the time to listen to what God is saying to us personally through the Bible.

"Be still and know that I am God." [110] He'll be waiting for you. And He's got something to say.

The Hail Mary

There are dozens if not hundreds of Marian prayers in the Catholic Church, such as the Salve Regina or the Memorare.[111] Yet while all of these are beautiful, the fundamental Marian

---

110 Psalm 46:11.
111 The Memorare was a favorite prayer of Mother Teresa. She would often resort to what she called her "Flying Novena:" praying nine Memorares for a particular intention. See, *Mother Teresa of Calcutta: A Personal Portrait*, Msgr Leo Maasburg, Ignatius Press (October 11, 2011).

prayer is, of course, the Hail Mary. I want to take a few pages to look at it.

The Hail Mary consists of three parts, two quotes from the Bible and the actual petition. It starts as follows:

> Hail, Mary, full of grace,
> the Lord is with thee.

This is the greeting of the angel Gabriel at the Annunciation. The Greek word that is translated "full of grace" is *kecharitoomene*. Although the root of the word, *charitoo* ("grace"), was fairly common, this form of the word[112] is unique in all of the Bible, and apparently in all of surviving Greek literature.

When we pray the Hail Mary, we mention Mary's given name of Mary. However, Gabriel did not include her name in his greeting. In the Greek, he says, "*Chaire,*

The Salve Regina

Hail, Holy Queen, Mother of Mercy, our life, our sweetness, and our hope. To you do we cry, poor banished children of Eve; to you do we send up our sighs, mourning and weeping in this vale of tears. Turn, then, most gracious Advocate, your eyes of mercy toward us; and, after our exile, show unto us the blessed fruit of your womb, Jesus. O clement, O loving, O sweet Virgin Mary, pray for us, O holy Mother of God, that we may be made worthy of the promisses of Christ. Amen.

The Memorare

Remember, O most gracious Virgin Mary, that never was it known that anyone who fled to your protection, implored your help, or sought your intercession was left unaided. Inspired by this confidence, I fly unto you, O Virgin of virgins, my mother; to you do I come, before you I stand, sinful and sorrowful. O mother of the Word Incarnate, despise not my petition, but in your mercy, hear and answer me. Amen.

---

112 Greek words can be very complex. A lot of our punctuation marks are fairly recent inventions. In ancient times, since so few people could read or write, things were added at the beginning and end of a word to show how the word fit into a sentence. Since they didn't have commas or semicolons or the like, the form of a word became terribly important.

kecharitoomene!" He is saying something like, "Hail, most blessed (or favored) one." He used the term more like a name, like, "Hail, Caesar!" It almost appears that *kecharitoomene* is the name for Mary used in Heaven.

In common usage, names are funny things. In and of themselves, names don't really mean anything in particular. They are arbitrary labels hung on people hopefully not scarring them for life. Through the way we live our lives, we give significance to our names. Our names do not give significance to us.

Names in the Bible are different. They signify something about the nature or role of the person. Adam means man or mankind because he is the father of mankind. Abram's name was changed to Abraham which means the father of many because God was going to make his descendants "as numerous as the stars in the sky." [113] And Jesus renamed Simon calling him Peter, the "Rock," because he would be the rock, the foundation stone on which He would build His Church. Names in the Bible tell us something fundamental about the person.

That is true of the Name of God Himself. When Moses asked God who he should say sent him to the Israelites, God revealed His name: "I Am Who Am." [114] God's name tells us that He is the only Person who exists in and of Himself. No one causes God. God simply exists. This is fundamental: God is existence itself. God's name tells us something about His very nature.

Gabriel's greeting to Mary also tells us something about Mary's nature. She is the blessed one, the favored one, the one who is full of grace like no other, so much so that in Heaven, that is how they

---

113 Gen. 26:4.
114 Ex. 3:14.

refer to her. And she is full of grace because the Lord is with her.

The second part of the Hail Mary is also a Bible verse:

> *Blessed art thou among women,*
> *and blessed is the fruit of thy womb, Jesus*

This is part of Elizabeth's greeting to Mary when she beheld Mary for the first time in her pregnancy. This is a truly wondrous moment. Mary was told that she would conceive a child who would be the Son of the Most High God. As proof, Gabriel told her that Elizabeth in her old age was miraculously in her sixth month. In her profound humility and love, Mary sets out to go to help Elizabeth. Traveling outside of a town in those days was a dangerous thing to do, but Mary went anyway. And she stayed with Elizabeth until John the Baptist was born.

Isn't that the way Mary is with us? As soon as we call on her, she rushes to our aid, heedless of her own safety or well-being, bringing us Jesus. She knows that He is the best medicine for whatever ails us.

And we, like Elizabeth, should be filled with wonder that the mother of Our Lord, the most blessed among women, should come to us. She said, "And how does this happen to me, that the mother of my Lord should come to me?" [115] Like Elizabeth, we should praise Mary for her profound faith in the word of God spoken to her by Gabriel. Elizabeth's response should be our own response.

The final part of the Hail Mary is the actual petition, which I recently read was added during the time of the Black Plague:

> *Holy Mary, Mother of God, pray for us sinners*
> *now and at the hour of our death.*

---

115 Luke 1:43.

Here we ask for Mary's prayers, particularly at the hour of our death.

I grew up in Texas. At that time, I was surrounded by well-meaning evangelical Christians. I often heard the criticism that "you Catholics worship Mary." I really had no response at the time. My parents were good Catholics. We went to Mass every Sunday as a family; my mother went to daily Mass when she could. But we didn't pray the Rosary at home as a family or talk much about our faith, much less about Mary. As I grew up, I kind of left Mary to the side so as not to offend my Protestant friends.

Many years later, that changed. I was going through a particularly tough time with work, bills were mounting, and I was quite desperate with a large family. I was driving home one night, and it occurred to me that I should pray a Rosary. I didn't have one in the car, and only vaguely remembered any of the mysteries, but that first night, I did the best I could. When I got home, I did some research and figured out how to pray the Rosary.

I have since come to know Mary as a very special person. I see evidence of this (and this is just my own personal observation) in the contrast between Gabriel's encounter with Mary and his encounter with Zacharias in the first chapter of the Gospel of Luke. When the angel Gabriel appeared to Zacharias to announce the birth of John the Baptist, he was very domineering. He lectured Zacharias, telling him that Elizabeth would have a child even though she was way beyond her child-bearing years. When Zacharias asked how this could be, Gabriel struck him dumb, mute. Gabriel, being a pure spirit, could see the disbelief of Zacharias.

In contrast, when Gabriel appeared to Mary at her home, he was deferential, respectful. Again, as a pure spirit, he could see that although Mary didn't understand, she was deferential and profoundly humble. He said, "Hail, favored one!" [116] He told her that she would be the mother of God. When Mary similarly asked, "How can this be?" [117] Gabriel very gently explained, even offering Elizabeth's pregnancy as proof. When Mary said, "May it be done to me according to your word," he left her in peace. Gabriel knew that Mary was special, she was the one blessed like no other.

One of my favorite stories in the Bible is the story of the wedding feast at Cana. [118] When the wine was running short, Mary turned to Jesus. She didn't ask Him to do anything. She just pointed out that they had no more wine. Jesus protested saying

> *Glory Be*
> *Glory be to the Father, and to the Son, and to the Holy Spirit. Amen*

> *The Apostles' Creed*
> *I believe in God, the Father almighty, Creator of Heaven and earth, and in Jesus Christ, His only Son, our Lord, who was conceived by the Holy Spirit, born of the Virgin Mary, suffered under Pontius Pilate, was crucified, died, and was buried; He descended into Hell; on the third day He rose again from the dead; He ascended into Heaven, and is seated at the right hand of God the Father almighty; from there He will come to judge the living and the dead. I believe in the Holy Spirit, the holy catholic Church, the communion of saints, and the forgiveness of sins, the resurrection of the body, and life everlasting. Amen.*

---

116 Luke 1:28.
117 Luke 1:34
118 John 2:1-10.

it wasn't yet His time. Mary completely ignored Him. Instead, she turned to the servers and said, "Do whatever He tells you."[119] Without questioning His mother, Jesus turned the water into wine, His first miracle. As Venerable Archbishop Fulton Sheen (†1979) once observed, this was the first step on the road to Calvary. Jesus couldn't (and He still can't) say no to His mother. We should regularly turn to her in our own needs.

The Rosary

As mentioned above, monks and nuns prayed the Psalms daily. The laity could not do that as many of them didn't know how to read. So, instead, they began to string "Hail Marys" together in prayer. Over time, they added Our Fathers, Glory Be's, and the Apostles' Creed. This became the Rosary.[120] Today the Church has incorporated the prayer of St. Mary Margaret Alacoque (the Miraculous Medal Prayer) and the Fatima Prayer.

> *Miraculous Medal Prayer*
> *Mary, conceived without sin, pray for us who have recourse.*

A full Rosary consists of four sets of mysteries (the Joyful, the Luminous, the Sorrowful, and the Glorious) prayed with five decades of Hail Marys introduced by an Our Father.

> *The Fatima Prayer*
> *O my Jesus, forgive us our sins, save us from the fires of Hell, lead all souls to Heaven, especially those who have the most need of your mercy. Amen*

- We begin with a statement of our faith, the Apostles Creed (but it can also be the Nicene Creed).

---

119 John 2:5 (Her last words in the Bible.)
120 The Rosary began as a medieval substitute for the Liturgy of the Hours that the monks and nuns would pray. CCC ¶2678.

- We then pray an Our Father.
- Next, we pray three Hail Marys, one for each of the theological virtues of faith, hope, and love.
- We then begin the decades praying an Our Father followed by the ten Hail Marys while meditating on the mysteries (see below) of our Lord's life.
- At the conclusion of each decade, we pray a Glory Be, the Miraculous Medal Prayer from St. Margaret Mary Alacoque, and the Fatima Prayer.
- After the fifth decade, we pray the Salve Regina (or in English, the "Hail Holy Queen") (mentioned above). And although it is not part of the tradition, I like to add the "Memorare" (also mentioned above).
- And then we state our intention(s) and ask Mary to pray for them.

When praying the Rosary, we reflect on the life of Jesus. There are four sets of these mysteries. Although the Rosary is viewed as a Marian devotion, it is also designed to help us to grow closer to the significant events of Our Lord during His life. By the grace of God, it was Mary who brought Jesus into the world to save us, and that is all she wants to do today in our daily lives. That is why we have the mysteries, as follows:[121]

The Joyful Mysteries
- The Annunciation
- The Visitation
- The Nativity
- The Presentation
- The Discovery of Jesus in the Temple

---

121 Scriptural references are provided in the Appendix.

The Luminous Mysteries

- The Baptism of Our Lord
- The Wedding at Cana
- The Proclamation of the Kingdom
- The Transfiguration
- The Last Supper

The Sorrowful Mysteries

- The Agony in the Garden
- The Scourging at the Pillar
- The Crown of Thorns
- Jesus is Made to Bear His Cross
- The Crucifixion

The Glorious Mysteries

- The Resurrection
- The Ascension
- Pentecost
- The Assumption
- The Coronation of Mary

So now I try to pray a Rosary just about every day. Typically it is in my car going to or from work. I am often distracted when I pray. Sure it would be best for me to pray the Rosary in a quiet place away from distractions, but as Pope Saint John XXIII once said, the only bad Rosary is the one we don't say. And the Rosary is a powerful prayer: Padre Pio (†1968)[122] used to refer to it as his "weapon."

In most parishes there are groups, sodalities, that are dedicated to praying to Mary for the salvation of the world. They regu-

---

122 I will return to Padre Pio in talking about the bearing wrongs patiently as a spiritual work of mercy.

larly pray the Rosary as a group. One such group is the Legion of Mary. Subject to the usual conditions, an indulgence (maybe even a plenary indulgence) is gained by the recitation of the Rosary as a group.

I am not going to say that praying the Rosary has turned everything around for me. Difficult times persist. But I think that through praying the Rosary I have grown closer to Jesus, and that is what we should be doing all the time anyway.[123]

The Mass

Simply stated, the Church teaches that the Mass is the highest form of prayer. But what does that really mean?

To understand the phrase, I think we need to review in detail what prayer is. I want to look at prayer in a more basic, foundational fashion.

---

123 To grow more in your understanding of Mary and her place in our lives, I recommend St. Louis de Montfort's *True Devotion to Mary*; and as a complement to St. Louis' work, *True Devotion to the Holy Spirit* by Archbishop Luiz M. Martinez.

The Legion of Mary is a lay apostolate in the Catholic Church dedicated to prayer and personal service with the goal to bring Mary to the world as the infallible means of winning the world for Jesus. Through their prayer and service, they seek to have the Person of our Lord once again seen and served by Mary, His Mother.

The Catechism defines an indulgence as "The Remission before God of the temporal punishment due to sin whose guilt has already been forgiven." (CCC Glossary) Although a sin may be forgiven, it still has consequences. We can look at a sin like a broken bone. Once it's healed, the muscles need to be rehabilitated. The temporal punishment is like that rehabilitation.

An indulgence can be partial "if it removes part of the temporal punishment due to sin" or it can be plenary "if it removes all punishment." (CCC Glossary)

Vocal Prayer

Prayer can be divided into two broad categories: vocal and silent. Vocal prayer can be divided into five (5) forms. The first form is perhaps the most basic: God help me! This is the prayer of *petition* or supplication.[124] We need something, and we realize (sometimes after a torturous journey) that only God can solve our problem.

Even though this may be the most basic form of prayer, it has some profoundly beautiful elements to it. It recognizes and acknowledges the right relationship between God and humanity: it acknowledges that He is God, the Creator of all Who sustains everything in being, Who provides for us, and ultimately Who loves us. Why would we think He would answer our prayers if He didn't love us? In the prayer of petition we acknowledge that we are mere creatures who are totally dependent on God. I actually think God loves it when we go to Him with all of our endless petitions.

The second form of vocal prayer is *intercession*.[125] This is where we pray for the needs of others. Like the prayer of petition, intercession acknowledges the right relationship between us and God, but we are asking for God's help for someone else. We're interceding for them. The prayer of intercession is an act of charity.

The third form of vocal prayer is *thanksgiving*.[126] Our prayer of petition or intercession may have been answered, or maybe God just dropped a gift, a grace, in our laps – like a beautiful sunset after a terrible storm – and we feel compelled to thank God.

---

124 CCC ¶¶2629-2633.
125 CCC ¶¶2634-2636.
126 CCC ¶¶2637-2638.

I suggest that the greatest prayer of thanksgiving is the one we pray in adversity – thanking God in spite of what's happened (more on that when we talk about suffering and sacrifice).[127]

The fourth form of vocal prayer is very similar to thanksgiving; it is the prayer of *praise*.[128] In this form of prayer, we simply praise God for Who He is, not so much for what He has given to us or others. I think many times our prayer of praise may be inseparably intertwined with our prayer of thanksgiving, but we can praise God without a specific reason or cause.

Although the Catechism doesn't recognize it as a separate form of vocal prayer, I would suggest one last form: *reparation*. This is the prayer of the penitent sinner: Lord, forgive me. A very good example of this is Psalm 51, King David's prayer of repentance. ("Have mercy on me, God, in your kindness".)

Silent Prayer

The second broad category of prayer is silent prayer. This would consist of Christ-centered meditation and contemplation.

Meditation is reflecting on something that helps us to grow more in our knowledge and love of God. It could be a Bible verse, a statue or a stained glass window, or simply a beautiful summer day. In any event, there is content.

Contemplation, on the other hand, is (to me, but I will, of course, defer to the masters on this) more of a moment in meditation when the object of our meditation simply slips away, and there

---

127 It seems to me that it is a natural human response to a beautiful sunrise or some wonderful event in our lives to want to give thanks. It occurred to me that it would be so sad to see something beautiful or to experience something wonderful and to have no one to thank for it.

128 The Catechism refers to this as the prayer of blessing and adoration while other sources refer to it as the prayer of praise. I kind of like the term praise here, so I decided to go with it. CCC ¶¶ 2626-2628

is just God. Spiritual writers will say that, whereas meditation is mediated by some "thing," contemplation is unmediated. Some writers argue that contemplation is a rare thing that is reserved only for "contemplative" monks and nuns. However, Fr. Thomas Dubay (†2010) argues forcefully that we are all called to contemplation which is a gift from God.[129] As I mentioned earlier when talking about prayer as a relationship, God can touch our souls directly without having to go through the senses. I believe that is what happens in contemplation. It is direct contact with God, and it is a gift.

But the one fundamental aspect of all prayer is that prayer is always an encounter between us and God. We need something for us or those we love, and we know that God is the only Person who can address that need; we are grateful to God for something He has given to us; we simply want to praise Him for Who He is; or we are simply trying to get to Know Him better, grow closer to Him. Prayer always involves an encounter with God.

The reason I speak of the Mass as "the highest form is prayer" is that all of these elements of prayer are present in the Mass. If we look at the prayers of Mass, we will see that there is petition for our needs; intercession for the needs of others, in fact for the whole world; thanksgiving for the many blessings God sheds upon us; praise simply because God is God; and at least meditation on the Word of God, if not even contemplation. And in all of these, we are encountering God. In fact, we are encountering God in an entirely unique and miraculous way. Jesus Christ, the second Person of the Holy Trinity, the Son of God, the Word through Whom all things were made, becomes present to us, Body, Blood,

---

129 *Prayer Primer*, Fr. Thomas Dubay, Ignatius Press (2002).

Soul, and Divinity, in the elements of the Eucharist. And further, if we are in a state of grace, we can receive Him bodily.

The Second Vatican Council referred to the Mass as the "source and summit" of our faith. At the Last Supper, Our Lord said, "I have eagerly desired to eat this Passover with you...." [130] He instructed us to "do this in memory of me." [131]

The Mass has been faithfully celebrated since the earliest days of the Church, in fact since the Last Supper. St. Paul talks about how he received the Eucharistic tradition from the Lord Himself.[132] In about the year 155, St. Justin Martyr (†165) wrote his *First Apology*. It contains a simple but rather detailed description of the Mass that sounds basically like the Sacrament we celebrate today.

But the Mass is even more than just the center of our worship as Catholics here on earth. It is our participation in the liturgy taking place in Heaven: there is a Mass in Heaven. We know that from the vision of St. John in the Book of Revelation. The vision occurs on the Lord's Day: "I was caught up in spirit on the Lord's day." [133] There is an altar; "I saw underneath the altar the souls of those who had been slaughtered because of the witness they bore to the word of God." [134] There is a Lamb (a symbol of Christ) that appears to have been slain: "Then I saw standing in the midst of the throne and the four living creatures and elders, a Lamb that seemed to have been slain.." [135] There are prayers offered throughout: "Each of the elders held a harp and gold bowls

---

130 Luke 22:15.
131 Luke 22:19.
132 1 Corinthians 11:23-26.
133 Rev. 1:10.
134 Rev. 8:3-5 and 11:1.
135 Revelation 6:9; see also 11:1.

filled with incense, which are the prayers of the holy ones." [136] So according to the Book of Revelation, there is a Mass in Heaven. [137]

On Calvary, Jesus sacrificed Himself for the salvation of the world. During His lifetime, He told us to follow Him. He told us that each day we must deny ourselves, take up our cross, and follow Him.[138] We are called daily to the Cross with Jesus. It is almost beyond belief, but Jesus wants us sacramentally to join Him on the Cross each and every day. And with Him, we are invited to offer our sacrifices to God the Father for the salvation of the world.

In receiving the Eucharist, we also become more like Jesus; we become more assimilated into the Body of Christ. By consuming the Body, Blood, Soul, and Divinity of our Lord and Savior, Jesus Christ, we become more like Him through the grace we receive. All of this is done through the Mass.

St. Pope Pius X (†1914), quoting from the Council of Trent (1545–1563), noted that the Eucharist is "the antidote whereby we may be freed from daily faults and be preserved from mortal sins." This Pope of the Blessed Sacrament, as he was often called, also said, "Holy Communion is the shortest and safest way to Heaven."

Fr. Andrew Apostoli in *Fatima for Today* noted that:

> *"We need the strength that Jesus gives us through our reception of him as our daily Bread to practice the virtues, to perform the works of mercy, to endure suffering and persecution, to conquer sin, and resist temptation."* [139]

---

136 Rev. 5:8; see also Rev. 8:3.
137 For a fuller discussion of this topic, see Scott Hahn, *The Lamb's Supper*, Doubleday, 1999,33
138 Luke 9:23.
139 *Fatima for Today*, Loc. 3160.

So at Mass, we are truly, profoundly present at the Last Supper; we are present at the foot of the Cross; as members of the Body of Christ, we are on the Cross with Jesus; and we are in Heaven. At Mass we receive grace which the Catechism defines as "The free and undeserved gift that God gives us to respond to our vocation to become his adopted children." [140] The grace we receive at Mass helps to form us more and more into the person God wants us to be: Christ-like. And that same grace empowers us to live our faith.

So why should we go to Mass? At Mass, we become more like Jesus. That will be really important on the Day of Judgment. When God the Father looks at me, I'd rather Him see Jesus, and not so much me. Also, when we are at Mass, we are literally present at the central event of all creation: the life, death, and resurrection of Jesus.

So in the end, my question is not why should we go to Mass? Rather, it's why would anyone want to miss Mass... ever?

Prayer Practices

We have looked at some of the fundamentals of prayer and some specific prayers, but now we should look at ways to practice prayer; how to begin.

Daily Prayer

It is only through regular prayer that we get to know God. To grow in our love of God, regular daily prayer is an absolute necessity. As I mentioned before, St. Francis de Sales said, we

---

140 CCC Glossary; grace is the favor God gives us to become partakers of the divine nature and eternal life (CCC ¶1996); it is participation in the very life of God (CCC ¶1997); it has been referred to as "deifying grace," the free gift "God makes to us of his own life, infused by the Holy Spirit into our soul to heal it of sin and to sanctify it." (CCC ¶1999.

should spend at least 30 minutes a day in prayer, or an hour if we're busy.

When my kids were younger, I was pretty busy. I would get caught up in all of the daily necessities I had in raising and providing for my family. Prayer could fall by the wayside in my world, so I had to figure out how to make it the central part of my day. We all need to develop a schedule so that prayer becomes a habit.

Start the morning with certain prayers such as the "Nicene Creed," the "Our Father," the "Hail Mary," the "Glory Be," the "Morning Offering" (discussed in the section on Sacrifice), the "Prayer to St. Michael" (see Appendix B), and/or the "Guardian Angel Prayer" (see Appendix B). Morning or noon Mass can fit into some people's schedules. Turn off the radio and listen to the Office of Readings on your phone on the way in to work, and pray the Rosary on the way home. Throughout the day, pray the "Jesus Prayer" and the "Morning Offering" to just keep God in mind.

And at the end of the day, take time to reflect on how God has been present in your life, give thanks for His blessings, and ask forgiveness for your failings. In a nutshell, this is the "Examen" of St. Ignatius (†1556), and it is a great way to end your day. Although similar to, it is not exactly an examination of conscience you would conduct in preparation for confession, but rather a spiritual review, an inventory, of the day.

An Ignatian Examen
- Ask God for the grace to pray.
- Review your day, looking for where God was present.
- Identify your blessings of that day, and give thanks.

- Identify your failings, ask forgiveness, and look for ways to improve.
- Resolve to follow God more closely tomorrow.
- Close with the Our Father.

And one last thing: an Act of Contrition. I once read that it is a good thing to end our day with an Act of Contrition. That makes sense.

I've heard people suggest that we should not pray for little things, but only big things. I disagree. God knows what we need before it even comes to our minds. But I think that He loves for us to go to Him and ask Him even for those little things. As I mentioned before, we are acknowledging that He is God and that we are totally dependent on Him. It is a little way to glorify God.

I've also heard people disparage routine or rote prayers. Again, I disagree. We need to be careful not to just mindlessly rattle off our prayers, but many of those memorized prayers consist of Bible verses or include some beautiful thoughts about God and His Saints. Taking the time to slowly, mindfully pray those routine prayers can be very beneficial, particularly when we don't know what to pray for.

One of the great masters of prayer is, of course, St. Teresa of Avila. In her book, *Interior Castle*, St. Theresa noted that although we can get caught up in just mindlessly reciting prayers, many times those routine prayers can lead to infused prayer, or contemplation. St. Theresa also outlined the phases (she refers to them as castles or mansions) of the development of prayer. I can't recommend the book enough. St. Theresa in particular is very down-to-earth. Another good book by her to read is *The*

Way of Perfection which consists of instructions on prayer that she gave to her nuns.

Because prayer is a relationship of love with the infinite God, it is extremely important to make it a part of our whole life; to let it surround us. A good handbook for developing and growing in prayer is *The Spiritual Exercises of St. Ignatius of Loyola.* I would also encourage readers to go to St. John of the Cross (†1591) to grow more in our relationship with God. In addition, we might consider several books by Fr. Thomas Dubay: *Prayer Primer*[141]; *Fire Within*[142]; and *Seeking Spiritual Direction.*[143]

Prayer is a relationship, and all relationships take time.[144] God wants a deep relationship with each of us through prayer. He is just waiting for us to invite Him. We need to develop a habit of prayer and take the time throughout the day to pray. And it seems to me to be a good trade to give up a little time here on earth to gain eternity in Heaven.

And in your mercy, please pray for the souls in Purgatory.

The Saints

Any soldier will tell you that probably the worst thing that can happen to you in battle is for you to be separated from your company, your fellow soldiers. Isolation can mean death; there is strength in numbers. In our spiritual battle, we should not (and do not need to) go it alone.

Jesus told us that we should pray for one another (Matthew 18:19), even for our enemies.[145] Paul in his epistles talks about

---

141 Fr. Thomas Dubay, Ignatius Press (2002).
142 *Fire Within*, by Fr. Thomas Dubay, S.M., Ignatius Press (1990).
143 Servant Press (1994).
144 *Christian Perfection and Contemplation: According to St. Thomas Aquinas and St. John of the Cross*, Fr. Reginald Garrigou-LaGrange, Tan Books (2010).
145 Matthew 5:44

how he prayed for the various churches he had founded.[146] He also asked for prayers for himself. [147] Jesus told us that He would be present whenever two or more are gathered in prayer. [148]

Praying for one another is common in every Christian faith tradition. Many conversations begin or end with, "Please pray for me," or "I'll keep you in my prayers." There's a long tradition of praying for one another in Christianity.

Although everyone's prayers are heard, we don't just ask anyone to pray for us. Instead, we usually would ask a minister, such as a priest in a Catholic parish or a minister in a Protestant church. Or we may ask someone who seems to be particularly close to God, a holy person. We probably assume (and with good reason[149]) that God will listen to that person's prayers.

In the Gospel of Mark, we have a story of the healing of a blind man. Jesus was in Bethsaida, and the residents brought Him a blind man and begged Him to heal him. Jesus took him outside the town, put spittle on his eyes, and laid His hands on him. When asked what he could see, he said, "I see people looking like trees and walking." So Jesus laid hands on him again, and he saw everything distinctly.[150]

This always struck me as an odd story. Why the gradual healing? Why did Jesus lay His hand on him twice? And why the spittle?

It wasn't until I recently heard a sermon about this story that it made some sense. It all focused on where Jesus was: Bethsaida. In two places in the Gospel, Jesus condemns the citizens of Bethsaida for their lack of faith.[151] So He apparently had to go out-

---

146 Colossians 1:9.

147 1 Thessalonians 5:25; Romans 15:30; Colossians 4:3.

148 Matthew 18:19.

149 Prov. 15:29; Psalm 34:18; 1 Peter 3:12; and Jas. 5:16b-18.

150 Mark 8:22-25.

151 Matthew 11:21 and Luke 10:13.

side of that faithless town and work through that faithlessness to perform the miracle. In a number of places in the Gospels, after Jesus has performed a miracle, He tells people that their faith has healed them or saved them. [152] So trust in God. Faith that God can answer our prayers is central, fundamental, even critical. So when we want our prayers answered, we ask people of faith, holy people, to pray for our intentions.

So if we asked holy people on earth to pray for us, why wouldn't we ask the Saints?

If you walk into any Catholic church, you can't help but notice the statues and stained glass windows, many of which depict the Saints. They're everywhere.

If we read the Book of Revelation, we see that the saints are in Heaven with God, even while there are men and women on earth. And what are the saints doing? Among other things, they are praying. In Chapter 5, it says, "Each of the elders held a harp and gold bowls filled with incense, which are the prayers of the holy ones." [153] So the saints in Heaven are offering prayers to God.

Why would the saints be praying in Heaven? The saints already have won the ultimate victory. We all want to be in Heaven, and they are already there. I think the only logical conclusion is that in addition to praising God, the saints in Heaven are praying for us here on earth. They are not indifferent to our needs.

Life on earth always involves some uncertainty. We need all the help we can get. The saints fought the good fight and won the crown. They didn't fight against creatures that could just kill them; they fought against powerful diabolical forces trying to

---

152 Matthew 9:22 and 29; Mark 5:34 and 10:52; and Luke 7:50, 8:48, and 18:42.
153 Revelation 5:8.

drag them to Hell for all eternity. And by the grace of God, they won. We certainly should ask them to pray for us!

Some people are concerned that when we are praying to the Saints for help, we are worshiping them, but that is not the case. The Church distinguishes between the honor that is due to the Saints and angels as the servants of God ("doulia" which comes the Greek word for slavery) and the worship that is due to God alone ("latria" which comes from the Greek word meaning worship or service). We owe the Saints honor because they have overcome the trials of this life and have been victorious in the battle. They should be our heroes.

And since they are in Heaven before God praying for us, it is only right that we ask them for their prayers. We have thousands of canonized Saints in the Church, although we can only celebrate maybe about 300 of them during a liturgical year. Certain Saints are closely associated with certain needs. For instance, St. Anthony of Padua (†1231) is the patron Saint of lost objects. St. Joseph is the patron Saint of workers, but also for the sale of a house. The parish priest St. John Vianney is the patron Saint of parish priests. The lawyer, St. Thomas More (†1535), is the patron Saint of lawyers. St. Peregrine (†1345) who suffered from cancer on his leg is the patron Saint of those suffering from cancer. St. Arnold of Soissons (†1087) is the patron Saint of brewers. St. Drogo of Sebourg (†1186) is the patron Saint of coffee shop owners. There are patron Saints for almost any need. They are recognized for their particular interest in that need. We should turn to them in our times of need or at any time we think of it.

We should learn about the Saints, find one that really appeals to us: maybe it's a mother or father who was a Saint; maybe it's a Saint who had to bear the same crosses we bear; maybe it's a bold, outspoken Saint; or a quiet, meek Saint. For those of us with family members who have fallen away from the Church, maybe a regular novena to St. Monica (†387) would be in order. She was the mother of St. Augustine who prayed for her son for years while he led a dissolute life. Or if you or a loved one is struggling with the scourge of pornography, I

A novena is a series of prayers said over the course of nine days typically requesting the prayers of a particular Saint for a particular purpose. Novenas are an ancient practice in the Church rooted in the instructions of our Lord to the disciples at his Ascension when He told them to return to Jerusalem and await the Holy Spirit during the nine days between the Ascension and Pentecost. The Novena to the Holy Spirit is still the only novena officially prescribed by the Church.

would suggest a novena to Maria Goretti (†1902). She died at the age of twelve (12) as the result of a sexual assault by a neighbor, saying that it was a sin that would lead him to Hell. Once we find a Saint or Saints, we should ask for their prayers and try to imitate their lives as much as we can in our current situations.

So make a Saint your hero! And then ask him or her to pray for you. As the writer of the Letter to the Hebrews says, we are surrounded by a cloud of witnesses,[154] so they are probably right beside us, just waiting to be asked. All they really want is for us to join them in Heaven.

Fasting

In America, people fast all of the time, although we don't call

---

154 Hebrews 12:1.

it that. We call it dieting. As most of us know, however, there is a religious aspect to fasting. After the Israelites made the golden calf and angered God, Moses fasted forty days and nights asking that God forgive them.[155] When disaster struck Israel, the prophet Joel called for a holy fast as a form of prayer to God.[156] When Jonah prophesied the destruction of Nineveh, the Ninevites fasted.[157] David fasted.[158] Elijah the prophet fasted.[159] Queen Esther fasted to save her people from destruction.[160] The Prophet Daniel fasted.[161]

Jesus Himself fasted. At the beginning of His ministry, after leaving the sheltered world of Nazareth and before going out to proclaim the Kingdom of God and confront the powers of Hell, Jesus went to the desert to pray, but also to fast.[162] Jesus, as the Second Person of the Trinity, did not need to pray or fast. However, when he became man, he emptied Himself of his Divinity.[163] In this case, as fully human, before undertaking His ministry, He fasted to set an example for us.

During Jesus's life, He did not ask the Apostles to fast.[164] But He did say that after His death, his disciples would fast: "The days will come when the bridegroom is taken away from them, and then they will fast." [165] In St. Paul's second letter to the Corinthians, he mentions his frequent fasts.[166] Many of the Church

---

155 Ex. 34:28; Deut. 9:9-18.
156 Joel 1:14-2:27.
157 Jonah 3:6-7.
158 2 Sam 12:16.
159 1 Kings 19:4-8.
160 Esth. 4:15-17.
161 Dan. 10:1-3.
162 Matt. 4:1-11; Luke 4:1-4.
163 Phil. 2:7.
164 Matt. 9:14-17.
165 Matt. 9:15.
166 2 Cor. 11:27.

Fathers – among them, Tertullian (†220), Origen (†254), St. Anthony (†356), Evagrius (†399), and St. Augustine – encouraged us to fast.

Almost universally, the Saints have encouraged us to fast. St. Francis of Assisi who is sometimes portrayed as a "flower child" fasted 40 days, seven times each year. Yes, the math works.

But you might ask why? In his Epistles, Paul uses the

> *The Catechism defines concupiscence as "Human appetites or desires which remain disordered due to the temporal consequences of original sin... which produce an inclination to sin." (CCC Glossary).*

term "flesh" to refer to the world of sin. He says that "flesh" and spirit are at odds with one another. [167] He tells us that to overcome our tendency to sin (our concupiscence, to echo St. Augustine), we need to mortify our bodies.[168] He himself said that he drove his body to train it lest he lose what he preached to others.[169] Fasting is a form of that mortification.

The Catechism also encourages us to fast. We are told that "[t]he way of perfection [necessarily] passes by way of the Cross. There is no holiness without renunciation and spiritual battle. Spiritual progress entails the ascesis[170] and mortification that gradually lead to living in the peace and joy of the Beatitudes ..." [171]

St. Basil the Great (†379) lived in the fourth century in Cappadocia, an inland area of present-day Turkey that is dry and arid. He was made the bishop of the area and preached such bold ser-

---

167 Gal. 5:17.
168 Rom 8:13.
169 1 Cor. 9:27.
170 The Catechism defines ascesis as "The practice of penance, mortification, and self-denial to promote greater self-mastery and to foster the way of perfection by embracing the way of the cross." CCC, Glossary. It is a Greek term that simply means "training."
171 CCC ¶ 2015.

mons that the Emperor in Constantinople banished him from his own diocese. He encouraged all of his flock to fast (referring to it in the feminine):

> *"Fasting gives birth to the prophets, she strengthens the powerful. Fasting makes lawmakers wise. She's a safeguard of the soul, a satisfying companion to the body, a weapon for the brave, a discipline for champions. Fasting knocks over temptations, anoints for godliness. She is a companion of sobriety, the crafter of a sound mind. In wars, she fights bravely. In peace, she teaches tranquility. She sanctifies the Nazirite, and she perfects the priest.*[172]

As I mentioned earlier, St. John of the Cross was a Spanish mystic who along with St. Teresa of Avila, helped to reform the Carmelite religious order and formed the religious order known as the Discalced Carmelites. He suffered greatly for his efforts, being locked in a dark cell not much bigger than a large closet for nine months; being fed almost nothing; and being brought out only to be whipped – and all of this by his fellow Carmelites. Out of this experience came his passionate religious poetry, the *Dark Night of the Soul* and the *Ascent of Mount Carmel*.

St. John grew to realize that in order to grow closer to God, we have to let go of the things of this world. We have to detach from those things. Holding on to them was like putting mud on a pane of glass, preventing God's light from shining through us. The following is a reflection often attributed to him from his classic work on the spiritual life, the *Dark Night of the Soul*:

> *"The soul that is attached to anything, however much good there may be in it, will not arrive at the liberty of divine union. For whether it be*

---

172 About Fasting, Sermon 1, section 6.

a strong wire rope or a slender and delicate thread that holds the bird,
it matters not, if it really holds it fast; for, until the cord be broken, the
bird cannot fly."

Detachment is critical to holiness. And fasting helps us to be detached from earthly things.

St. Thomas Aquinas said there are three purposes for fasting. First, it is to bridle lust. Quoting from Augustine, he says that we can't lust if we are really hungry (that's a paraphrase, but I think it makes the point). The second reason to fast is that it sets us free for prayer. He refers to it as contemplation. The third reason to fast is in reparation for sins, both our own, but also for those of the whole world.[173]

Fasting is a powerful spiritual tool. In a way, it makes prayer physical. We as humans are composed of both a body and a soul (hence the resurrection of the body), and we should use our body in prayer through fasting. It strengthens us to resist temptation and to keep our eyes on God. As St. Paul repeatedly says, just as an athlete trains to compete for a crown, we fast to train our bodies and our souls to prepare for the spiritual combat we will face.[174]

Fasting also helps us to gain focus and clarity in our spiritual lives. I think a good analogy for this is a forest. In the spring and summer, when the leaves are on the trees, if we walk in the forest, we can only see a very limited distance. However, in the fall, and particularly in the winter, when the leaves are off the trees, we can see a great distance in the forest. It is that way with fasting. When we fast, we can push a lot of distractions out of the

---

173 *Summa Theologiae*, Question 147, Article 1, Answer.
174 Heb. 12:1; Phil 1:27-30, 2:16-18, and 2:28-30; Gal. 2:2; 1 Cor. 9:24-26; 1 Thes. 2:19; Col 5:7; Rom 11:11; 1 Tim. 4:7; 1 Tim. 6:12; and 2 Tim. 2:5.

way to focus on God. And by fasting and abstaining, we also tell God that we love Him for Him alone and not for any of the things that He gives us.

So, fast for yourself; fast for your family; fast for the Church; fast for the entire world. [175]

Chapel Visits

When I was a teenager, growing up in Austin, Texas, Father Charles Elmer was the pastor at our parish, St. Theresa's. Although I didn't know it at the time, during World War II, he had fought in the Battle of the Bulge. He had terrible asthma and had to sleep sitting up. He was one of the kindest, most generous men I've ever known.

Once he was talking about a trip he had to take to a neighboring town. It was maybe 45 minutes away. More than two hours before his meeting, he said that he had to get going. I pointed out that he had plenty of time, but he objected and told me that he didn't because there were several churches along the way. I asked him why that mattered. He told me that he never passed a Catholic Church without stopping in. Being an impatient teenager, I could see no sense in this. I asked him why he would do that, since he already had a church and that would just slow him down. With a kind of smile in his eyes, he said, "I just want to make sure that Jesus remembers me on the day of the Resurrection."

It is an amazing thing to think that Jesus Christ, the Word through Whom all things were made, the Lord of the universe, our King and our Savior, sits in the tabernacle of every Catholic Church around the world.

---

175 For a good current discussion on fasting, see Fr. Charles M. Murphy, *The Spirituality of Fasting: Rediscovering a Christian Practice*, Ave Maria Press, 2010.

And what is He doing? He's waiting. He's waiting for you and me to stop by. Although He already knows everything that we need, He's waiting for us to come and tell Him what we think we need. He's waiting for us to take a moment of the day that is His gift to us and give that small moment back to Him. He's waiting for us to just make the effort to drop by and say "Hi."

And when we do drop by, He is like the father in the parable of the Prodigal Son. He will lavish His grace on us. Yes, He will answer all of our prayers, but in His own way, and on His own schedule in a way that will be best for us. But rest assured, He will answer all of our prayers. In addition, He will draw each of us ever closer to Him, which is really our ultimate (perhaps unspoken or even unconscious) desire. He will fill that emptiness at the root of our being that was caused by Original Sin.

And when we drop by a church (or really anytime for that matter), we might want to pray a spiritual communion:

> *O my Jesus,*
> *I believe that you are truly present in the Most Holy Sacrament.*
> *I love you above all things,*
> *And I desire to receive you into my soul.*
> *Since I cannot at this moment receive you sacramentally,*
> *Come at least spiritually into my heart.*
> *I embrace You as if You were already there*
> *And unite myself wholly to You.*
> *Never permit me to be separated from You.*
> *Amen.*

So a visit to a church is an immensely powerful prayer. God is truly present there, just waiting. I can think of no better place to pray.

A Word About Grace

Before concluding this section on prayer, it might be helpful to say a word about the grace of God. It is all grace. Grace underlies everything in our spiritual journey. It is a grace to be moved to search for God in our lives. It is a grace to be moved to pray. It is a grace to love God so much that we want to flee from sin and even to avoid the near occasion of sin. It is a grace to want to help others in need. And it is the loss of grace that actually makes sin so horrible.

The Catechism distinguishes between "sanctifying grace" and "actual grace." *Sanctifying grace* is "[t]he grace that heals our human nature wounded by sin by giving us a share in the divine life of the Trinity." [176] It bestows on us the power to live as the children of God.

Actual graces are the little nudges that God gives us along the way, even on a daily basis, to help us to know and do His will. In the words of the Catechism, actual graces "refer to God's interventions, whether at the beginning of conversion or in the course of the work of sanctification." [177]

So in our prayer, we should pray for the grace of God to live our lives according to the will of God. It may be the best prayer we ever pray.

---

176 CCC Glossary.
177 CCC ¶2000.

PART THREE

Holiness

"Be holy because I am holy."[178]

---

178 1 Peter 1:16; Leviticus 11:44, 19:2, and 20:7 and 26.

What is Holiness?

We have now looked at prayer. But as St. James tells us, "The fervent prayer of a righteous person is very powerful." [179] So in order to make our prayer truly effective, we need to look at *righteousness*, or holiness.

Christians universally are called to holiness. [180] In fact, we are told that the unjust will not inherit the Kingdom of God, Heaven.[181] In addition, without holiness, no one will see the Lord.[182]

But that raises the question: what is holiness? The Bible tells us that there is no one holy like the Lord.[183] In the truest sense of the word, only God is holy.[184]

The problem, though, is that but for His revelation to us, God is unknowable. We should not presume to know what holiness is. As the philosopher Mircea Eliade (†1986) explains,[185] God is totally other. Being infinite, He is simply incomprehensible to us in our limited intellects. And God is the perfection, the completion, the fulfillment of everything, including holiness.

So how are we to be holy if we don't know what holiness is? I do not believe that holiness is just a set of rules or laws that we have to follow. Someone suggested to me that a good definition of holiness is from the Baltimore Catechism: "God made me to know Him, to love Him, and to serve Him in this world and to be

---

179 James 5:16.
180 Lev. 11:44–45; Lev. 19:2; Lev. 20:7 and 26; and Matt. 5:48.
181 1 Cor. 6:9-11.
182 Heb. 12:14.
183 1 Sam. 2:2.
184 Rev. 15:4.
185 See, *The Sacred and the Profane: The Nature of Religion*, pp. 9-10, Harper Torch Books (2015).

happy with Him forever in Heaven." [186] It seems that this tells us the "how" but not the "what" of holiness.

It does not appear that the Bible defines holiness per se. Rather, it is demonstrated by example. "The Word [Jesus Christ] became flesh to be our model of holiness." [187] And "[b]y his obedience to Mary and Joseph, as well as by his humble work during the long years in Nazareth, Jesus gives us the example of holiness in the daily life of family and work." [188]

There are several passages in St. Paul's letters where Paul talks about the characteristics of holiness: God's children must have heartfelt compassion, kindness, humility, gentleness and patience, bearing with one another and forgiving one another. [189] They must pursue righteousness, devotion, faith, love, patience, and gentleness. [190] In Christians, the Spirit of God produces love, joy, peace, patience, kindness, generosity, faithfulness, gentleness, and self-control. [191]

But as the Catechism points out, charity is the soul of holiness to which we are all called: it governs, shapes, and perfects all the means of sanctification. [192] The Catechism goes on quoting St. Theresa of Lisieux who said that love is the moving force enabling all members of the Church *to act*. Love is the vocation that includes all others. "It's a universe all its own, comprising all time and space – it's universal." [193] We are also told that holiness is the perfection of charity, or conversely, perfect charity

---

186 Baltimore Catechism No. 3, Lesson 1, Q. 150.
187 CCC ¶ 459.
188 CCC ¶ 564.
189 Col. 3:12-13.
190 1 Tim. 6:11.
191 Gal. 5:2223.
192 CCC ¶ 826, quoting from Lumen Gentium #42; Col. 3:14.
193 St. Therese of Lisieux, *Autobiography of a Saint*, tr. Ronald Knox (London: Havrill, 1958), p. 235, quoted in CCC Ibid...

constitutes holiness.[194] In summary, we could say that holiness is selfless-love as modeled by our Lord and Savior, Jesus Christ. And that makes sense, since God is love.[195]

What is Sin?

God has called us all to holiness[196] so that we may have life.[197] Since Jesus Christ is the perfect revelation, the perfect expression of the Father, we are called to be imitators of Christ.[198] Since nothing exists outside of God, reality only exists in and through God. That being the case, then only what is truly real is what is holy. Or saying that another way, true reality is what is holy.

The opposite of holiness is evil, the absence of good.[199] Evil is a very odd thing. God is the Creator of all things. The only things that exist are things created and sustained in being by God. Since God is all good, the Church understands that He did not create anything that is evil. Evil is actually the absence of the good that should be present. So from a certain perspective, evil, in and of itself, does not exist. But we have all experienced evil, so what is it?

"Moral evil ... results from the free choice to sin ...." [200] To understand sin, I think it is helpful to reflect on God. God is love. All God wants from us is selfless love like He loves us. We all know that love has to be free or it is a fraud, a mockery. Forced love is not love. So God had to give us free will. He has given us the freedom not to love Him. He has given us the freedom to sin.

---

194 CCC ¶1709.
195 1 John 4:8.
196 1 Thess. 4:7.
197 Amos 5:14.
198 Eph. 5:1.
199 CCC, Definitions, *Evil*.
200 Id. (cf. CCC ¶311).

According to St. Thomas Aquinas, sin is an act that is contrary to reason informed by the law of God.[201] God has made us subject to His law which we know through the dictates of our conscience, and we must conform to His dictates. Otherwise, we commit sin.[202] In effect, sin is performing some act that is contrary to God's intended purpose. Since God and His will are the only reality, and sin is an act contrary to God's intended purpose, sin is an act of the unreal that leads us away from God. Sin leads to nothing and wastes the precious gift of our time and our lives.

Throughout his letters, St. Paul admonishes his flock to avoid sin. He pleads with them to offer themselves as living, holy, and pleasing to God.[203] He tells them to purify themselves from sin.[204] Paul tells us we must "put to death" all immorality, impurity, passion, evil desire, and the greed that is idolatry.[205]

It seems that in contemporary America, very few people pay much attention to the reality or even the possibility of sin. Sin is thought of, if at all, as a kind of archaic, old-fashioned concept. It's something we were taught about as children, but it was just a way to keep us in line, nothing more.

But it doesn't appear that God views sin in that way. The Incarnation should tell us something about how God looks at sin. God is infinite. He is perfect in everything. God is perfectly complete in Heaven. He has no need of anything else from any of us. He is surrounded by a myriad of angels praising Him and glorifying Him. He is perfect in love and in complete joy. Human beings do not add to God's perfection, His love, or His joy, and yet while

---

201 St. Thomas Aquinas, *De malo*, 7:3.
202 Rom. 14:23.
203 Rom. 12:1.
204 2 Cor. 7:1.
205 Col. 3:5.

our existence is nothing compared to His, He loves us beyond imagining and shares His life with us.

Yet, Jesus Christ, the Second Person of the Holy Trinity, Who is Himself God, emptied Himself of his divinity[206] and became man. He lived among us, suffered His Passion, and died a painful and humiliating death all to redeem us.

If sin is such a minor thing, why would God feel it necessary and appropriate to go through that? The question this should raise for all of us is how horrible must sin be for God to have to do that?

Throughout the Bible, God tells us to root out sin. In the Old Testament, He ordered the Israelites to destroy the pagan nations in order to completely root out the pollution of pagan idolatry and to destroy all pagan worship practices.[207] He told them to utterly destroy the cities they invaded. [208]

It's important to look at these directives from a spiritual perspective, not per se literally. It wasn't that God wanted to destroy people; He wanted to eliminate all sinful influences that could entrap the Israelites and ultimately lead them to spiritual death.[209] God wanted to eliminate all of the surrounding pagans "so that they do not teach you to do all the abominations that they do for their gods, and you thus sin against the LORD, your God." [210]

But the Israelites did not wipe out the pagan nations where they invaded as God told them, and after the time of David, the

---

206 Philippians 2:7.
207 Deut. 7:2, 5, 12:2-3; Ex. 34:12-13; and Judges 2:1-2.
208 Deut. 7:1-5, 20:16-18.
209 Deut. 7:16; Ex. 23:33; Jos. 23:13; and Judges 2:3.
210 Deut. 20:18.

Jews adopted the pagan ways. They practiced pagan worship.[211] They imitated their abominable practices,[212] including child sacrifice.[213] After many warnings from the prophets, God allowed the northern 10 tribes to be invaded and taken by the Assyrians in 722 BC. And then the southern two tribes were attacked by the Babylonians around 605 BC. And then beginning in 597 BC, many in the southern kingdom were deported to Babylon for approximately 70 years.

Sin is a serious matter to God. On March 15, 1937, St, Faustina spiritually experienced the bitterness of the passion of Christ. She later wrote: "I learned how horrible sin was. God gave me to know the whole hideousness of sin. I learned in the depths of my soul how horrible sin was, even the smallest sin, and how much it tormented the soul of Jesus."[214] God wants us to do almost anything to root it out. God's call has been consistent from the Old Testament to the New: "Be holy because I [am] holy."[215]

Mortal Sin

Relativism is a world view. It is a philosophy that rejects any moral absolutes. It is the belief that there are no absolute truths, only the truths that a particular individual or culture chooses to believe. Under relativism, different people can have different views about what is good and what is bad. What's good for you is not necessarily good for me, and what's bad for you isn't necessarily bad for me. Morality is what I make it to be. But that is not what the Bible or the Church teach.

---

211 Judges 2:1-2; 1 Kings 11:5.
212 Ez. 8-11.
213 2 Kings 16:3-4; and Psalm 106:34-39.
214 *Divine Mercy in My Soul Diary of Saint Maria Faustina Kowalska*, ¶ 1016, Marian Press (2914)
215 1 Peter 1:16; Leviticus 11:44, 19:2, and 20:7 and 26.

In the Bible, St. John in his first epistle distinguishes between what we would call venial sins, and those that he calls "deadly" or mortal. He says, "There is such a thing as deadly sin .... All wrongdoing is sin, but there is a sin that is not deadly." [216]

Although the Church does not actually have a list of mortal sins, the Catechism teaches that for a sin to be mortal, three conditions have to be present[217]:

- grave matter;
- full knowledge; and
- deliberate consent.

These are grave offenses against the love of God, either directly or indirectly.

Mortal sin is where we knowingly and completely reject the love and mercy of God to such an extent that we direct our lives away from the blessedness of God. St. Thomas Aquinas wrote that mortal sin is "when the will is directed to a thing that is in itself contrary to charity, whereby man is directed to his last end ...." [218] Through mortal sin we isolate ourselves by directing our lives toward things that are not God. If Heaven is eternal blessedness with God, then through mortal sin we direct ourselves, our destiny, to Hell.

The Horror of Mortal Sins

Starting back in the 1700s with St. Alphonsus Liguori, and continuing until the Second Vatican Council or so, the Redemptorist Order preached Lenten retreats on the Last Four Things: death, judgment, Hell, and Heaven. We don't talk much about Hell any-

---

216 1 John 5:16–17.
217 CCC ¶1857.
218 St. Thomas Aquinas, *Summa Theologiae*, Prima Secundae Partis, Q88, 2, corp. art., http://www.newadvent.org/summa/2088.htm#article 2.

more, but since Jesus repeatedly warned us about it, we have to believe in it. So, what is Hell?

In a vision given to St. Teresa of Avila, the great Spanish mystic and now a Doctor of the Church, Our Lord showed Teresa the place in Hell that had been reserved for her if she had not reformed her life.[219] Yes, there was fire. Yes, there were demons. Yes, she would have been confined in a very small space. Yes, there would have been pathetic, miserable screaming and cursing of God. There would have been no hope of ever getting out.

> *The Redemptorist Order was founded by St. Alphonsus Liguori to conduct missionary work initially among the neglected people in the countryside surrounding Naples. It has grown to an international religious order providing missions, retreats, and spiritual exercises.*

But what stood out most to me in her description was the isolation. "All this [the physical torment] was even pleasant to behold in comparison to what I felt.... These sufferings were nothing in comparison with the anguish of my soul, a sense of oppression, of stifling, and of pain so keen, accompanied by so hopeless and cruel affliction, that I know not how to speak of it." [220]

God is a community of Persons: Father, Son, and Holy Spirit. We are invited to join that Community as part of the Body of Christ. We need to recognize that that community is physically manifested in the world in the Catholic Church. We need to accept Jesus' invitation that He has extended to us to become a part of His world, the only reality that truly exists.

---

219 Teresa of Avila, *The Autobiography of Teresa of Avila*, p. 173, Kindle, independently published (2017).
220 Ibid. p. 174.

If we reject that invitation, we are powerless to do anything else. Because we have rejected the only real option which is God, we are left with nothingness. We cannot on our own unite into a community of any type.

We can see this to a certain extent in our daily lives here on earth. When we are with our family or friends, at the store, in a park, or even at a crowded party, we are in a very real sense still alone. Our experiences are our own, and we really don't share the reality of those experiences with other people. We try to share our human experiences (we try to bridge that gap) through conversation, poetry, music, and the like, but in the end we are still basically on our own. I could be standing right next to my wife looking at a rainbow, but the two of us would experience that rainbow in very different ways. I may be having a conversation with a close friend, but we will both be experiencing that conversation from our separate perspectives. We are all alone.

We seem to believe that there is some bond that connects us to other people. Perhaps Carl Jung (†1961), the pioneer psychologist, was right when he suggested that there is some sort of a collective unconscious. If so, it is not evident; it is subconscious. But if we cut ourselves off from God and others, I think that we break whatever connection we might have.

It occurred to me that there may be a good analogy of what the isolation of Hell will be like. Imagine, if you will, that you were to wake up in a coffin six feet under the ground with no escape. It would be a virtually hopeless situation. There would be no light; only darkness. Even if you had been buried with a watch on, it would only mock you since the passage of time would be meaningless. The only escape would be death. In the meantime, there would be darkness, hunger, thirst, claustrophobia, and desperation.

I would imagine that Hell will be something like that, except that there would be no escape. Death would not be a release since Hell is eternal.

That is Hell: to be profoundly alone with no hope for all of eternity. We may be surrounded by demons and other horrible sinners, but I think they will only intensify that feeling of isolation. And although some have argued that Hell is temporary,[221] the Church, in accord with Jesus, asserts that it is eternal.[222]

And the way we get to Hell is by committing mortal sin, completely rejecting the love of God in our lives. Since God is love, and all He really wants is for us to be in Heaven with Him, mortal sin is the greatest tragedy in the universe, both visible and invisible.

When people encountered Jesus, they would many times recognize something divine about Him, although they may not have known Him. Mortal sin can blind us so that we can't recognize God even though He is always right beside us.

Venial Sins

But what about venial sins? These are the little sins we commit every day: little white lies; fudging on some project at work; inflating our expense account; talking about people behind their backs; driving uncharitably; those minor things we do where "no one is really hurt." How serious can those really be?

The problem, of course, is that Jesus told us that we should be

---

221 This is pretty technical, but the 3rd century theologian Origen taught something called "apokatastasis." Based on Colossians 1:20 (and to a lesser extent Ephesians 1:10), he felt that Hell would eventually end, and all of creation would be reunited in Heaven with God. Based on the teachings of Christ, the Church rejected that assertion. Hell is forever. That belief is one of the reasons that Origen was not declared to be a Saint.

222 CCC ¶ 1035.

perfect even as Our Heavenly Father is perfect.[223] That is further complicated if we think about the perfection of God. Jesus also warned us against presuming that the way to Heaven is easy:

> *"Enter through the narrow gate; for the gate is wide and the road broad that leads to destruction, and those who enter through it are many. How narrow the gate and constricted the road that leads to life. And those who find it are few."* [224]

I believe that in our contemporary Church, and even more so in our society, we try to over-humanize Jesus. Yes, He is True God and True Man, but we seem to downplay the Divine Nature of Jesus. We like to think of Him more as a great moral teacher.

But it is a serious error to ignore or even just minimize the Divine. In our reflection on sin, we need to keep in mind that God is the perfection of all perfections. He is perfect in love beyond anything that we can ever imagine. He is perfect in beauty beyond anything we can possibly envision. And yes, He is perfect in holiness beyond anything we can ever possibly conceive. And it is that perfect holiness that makes even venial sins so horrible.

In a series of lectures that have been published under the title *Anglican Difficulties*, Blessed John Cardinal Newman (†1890) wrote:

> *"The Church holds that it were better for the Sun and Moon to drop from Heaven, for the Earth itself to fall, and for all the many millions who are on it to die of starvation, in extremist agony (as far as temporal affliction goes), than that one soul, I would not say would be lost, but should commit one venial sin."* [225]

In the introduction to a little pamphlet entitled simply *Venial*

---

223 Matt. 5:48.
224 Matt. 7:13-14; see also Luke 13:22-30.
225 *Anglican Difficulties*, P. 199.

Sin[226] by Bishop John S. Vaughan (†1925), the Benedictine Cardinal Gasquet related a little observation: "St. Catherine of Siena, when she was shown how hideous venial sin made the soul in God's sight, [she] fainted at the vision."

Yet as Bishop Vaughan went on to write, we don't seem to appreciate the gravity of venial sin, because the consequences are not as apparent as those of mortal sin. In his treatise, Bishop Vaughan points out at least four consequences of venial sin.

First, venial sin tends to darken the intellect and cloud the judgment regarding the things of God. We lose a sense of the holiness of God and of His unapproachable sanctity. We see God more on the level of man, and less as the profoundly transcendent Being that He is. This spiritual blindness causes us to minimize the evil of venial sin.

A second consequence of venial sin is that the habit of continual venial sins "increases the violence and strength of our spiritual enemies," our own passions, sinful desires, and evil intentions.[227] Bishop Vaughan explains that "[s]mall passions easily grow by little indulgences, until they become almost irresistible." [228]

A third consequence of venial sin is that it weakens our friendship with God.[229] God is always waiting for us to turn to Him, but it is we who turn away from Him through our sins. When we turn away from God, we forfeit the close union to Him, which is what we should all be striving after.

Finally, Bishop Vaughan says that the fourth consequence of venial sin is that it disfigures us. We were created in the image

---

226 Tradibooks (2008).
227 *Venial Sins*, Loc. 485.
228 Ibid. Loc. 499.
229 Ibid. Loc. 513.

and likeness of God, who is transcendently beautiful. When we sin, we splatter our souls with what Bishop Vaughan calls unsightly filth. We stain it; we wound it; we render it so unsightly and hideous that we cannot enter the Presence of God without a thorough purging. To a certain extent, venial sin strips us of holiness.

Many in our society would like for us to look at sin – any sin – as being a mere personal failing and no more. People like to think that they are free agents in the world.

But I would challenge any of them to give up a sinful behavior for a month ... or maybe for 2 weeks ... or maybe just a week ... or maybe just for a couple of days. I think that they will find that they become almost consumed with thinking about whatever it is that they are trying to avoid. Everything they see or hear, and everywhere they turn, they will be reminded of that sinful habit. Sin does not make us free. I think that this must be a lot like trying to give up an addictive drug. Drug addicts feel as if they need the drug to stay alive when it is actually killing them. It is the same with sin.

Although our culture will tell us that sin sets us free, the Bible and the Saints often say how sin enslaves us. But what does that mean?

If some random person tells us to do something, we are free to tell him or her no. If an employer tells us to do something, we could always tell them no as well. We might be looking for a job the next day, but we could still say no.

"No" is not a real option for an addict. He or she can't say no without real, serious consequences. And there would be no escaping from those consequences.

It is like that with any habitual sin. We may try to say no, but the attraction of that sin grows and grows until it is almost irresistible. That is why our sinfulness is like an addiction.

Jesus told his disciples that whoever sees Him sees His Father.[230] It's as if Jesus wanted to be transparent, a window to the Father. You and I are called to be like windows to Jesus so that when people look at us, they see Jesus. Sin ... even venial sin ... clouds that view, it makes that window dirty. We need to avoid that.

The good news, of course, is that we have a remedy for those sins already committed: confession and penance.[231] But in order for confession to be truly effective, we must resolve to try to avoid those sins in the future. Will we sin again? Unfortunately, yes, and it may (probably certainly) even be the same sin. Still, we need to keep going back to confession and doing penance. This is how we strengthen our moral resolve and grow in holiness.

The Ten Commandments

When Moses was preparing to die, he called the Israelites together and talked to them one last time. He told them that he had put before them the choices of life and death. He told them that if they obeyed God and followed His commandments, they would live and grow numerous, and the Lord would bless them in the land He was giving to them. But he warned them that if their hearts were turned away and they did not obey God and were led astray, they would certainly perish. They would not have a long life in the land that He was giving to them. He told them to choose

---

230 John 12:45.
231 Mother Angelica, the founder of EWTN, once said that she went to confession every week. She did not want to have to explain more than one week when she faced God on her death.

life by loving the Lord and obeying His commandments.[232]

God gave us this basic moral code. The problem, though, is that most Americans see the Ten Commandments (if they think of them at all) as a nice set of moral suggestions, maybe a little old-fashioned and out of step with the times.

Fear of the Lord

I think they are much more than that. It is an arrogance, a pride, a hubris (as the Greeks called it) for us to dismiss the will of God and substitute our own will, and that is precisely what we do when we dismiss the Ten Commandments.

Throughout the Old Testament there is a phrase that pops up: "fear of the Lord." The Psalmist tells us that "The fear of the LORD is the beginning of wisdom." [233] The Book of Proverbs repeatedly tells us the same.[234] The Catechism teaches that fear of the Lord is one of the gifts of the Holy Spirit. [235]

But we shouldn't understand this "fear" as in horror, such as the reaction of characters in a horror movie. That is referred to as servile fear, the fear of a slave regarding his or her master. Rather, this is an awe or a deep and profound respect and reverence for an all-loving but also all-powerful Father. We should not casually dismiss the Ten Commandments and substitute our own will. We are not God no matter how much we may rebel against that idea. God is the only reality. And our humble submission to the loving will of God is the fear of the Lord.

The Prophet Isaiah in describing the promised Messiah says he will be filled with a spirit of fear of the Lord.[236] Jesus said that

---

232 Dt. 30:15-20; 26:16-19.
233 Psalm 111:10.
234 Proverbs 9:10, 15:33, and 1:7.
235 CCC ¶1831.
236 Is, 11:2.

He did not come to abolish the Commandments but to fulfill them: "Do not think that I have come to abolish the law or the prophets. I have come not to abolish but to fulfill." [237] In addition, He warned, "whoever breaks one of the least of these commandments and teaches others to do so will be called least in the kingdom of Heaven." [238] Jesus told us that we would remain in His love if we keep His commandments.[239] St. John tells us that the way we love God is by keeping His commandments: "For the love of God is this, that we keep his commandments." [240] The Church teaches that we are to live by the Commandments: the Ten Commandments "are fundamentally immutable, and they oblige always and everywhere. No one can be dispensed from them. The Ten Commandments are engraved by God in the human heart."[241] Yet though we are supposed to live by these Commandments, I wonder how many of us can even name them.

When Jesus was asked what the greatest Commandment is, He gave two: love God with your whole heart, with your whole soul, and with your whole mind; and love your neighbor as yourself.[242] Holiness is truly selfless love (like the love of Christ on the Cross), and holiness has two dimensions: love of God and love of our neighbor. Just as the first three petitions in the Our Father are about God, the first three Commandments are about God. The rest of the Commandments deal more with our relations with each other.

What follows is just a series of reflections on the Ten Com-

---

237 Matt. 5:17
238 Matt. 5:19
239 John 15:10.
240 1 John 5:3.
241 CCC ¶¶ 2072.
242 Matt. 22:37-40; cf. Mark 12:28-34 and Luke 10:25-28.

mandments. You'll notice that I grouped the Sixth Commandment with the Ninth, and the Seventh Commandment with the
Tenth. I have seen that done in several examinations of conscience, and I thought that it made sense because of their nature. I think it works. I hope you agree.

Although we tend to look at the Ten Commandments as a set of
legal rules for us to follow, I think that it is better to look at them
as instructions on loving selflessly. As I mentioned, holiness is
selfless love. God has called us to be perfect even as He is perfect.
The Ten Commandments are part of that.

The First Commandment [243]

*"You Shall Worship the Lord Your God
And Him Only Shall You Serve."*

If you ask most Americans if they have idols in their lives, they
will probably look at you as if you were speaking a foreign language. When we think of idols (if we ever do), we might think of
rock stars or movie stars. I'm not sure that we actually idolize
them so much as envy them. But if we talk about an idol we worship, we think of golden statues in the Old Testament or maybe
Greek or Roman gods, but we believe we are too modern for that
sort of superstitious thing.

But an idol does not have to be a statue. An idol is anything on
which we center our lives. It could be money or power or fame
or pleasure. If our lives are centered on some created thing, that
thing is an idol. And I would argue that we choose our idols because they allow us to do what we want to do. In a sense, our
fundamental idol is ourselves.

---

243 CCC ¶¶ 2084-2141

And if we have an idol, we have some sort of a religion. If we look at religion as a set of rules or guiding principles that help us to achieve our ultimate happiness, then the religion of most Americans is freedom. If we are free to do whatever makes us happy, whatever fulfills us, then we are our own "god" in this "Religion of Freedom." We are free to set the rules (relativism) to reach our fulfillment, our destiny.

In her *Dialogue*, St. Catherine of Siena recounts how Jesus told her, "You know that every evil is founded in self-love, and that self-love is a cloud that takes away the light of reason, which reason holds in itself the light of faith ...." [244]

It seems to me that this self-love, this self-worship is at the heart of all of our sins, including Original Sin. Look at the dialogue between Eve[245] and Satan in Genesis.

> Satan: *"Did God really say, 'You shall not eat from any of the trees in the garden?"*
>
> Eve: *"We may eat of the fruit of the trees in the garden; it is only about the fruit of the tree in the middle of the garden that God said, 'You shall not eat it or even touch it, or else you will die."*
>
> Satan: *"You certainly will not die! God knows well that when you eat of it your eyes will be opened and **you will be like gods**, who know good and evil."* [246]
>
> *"You will be like gods."*

---

244 Catherine of Siena, *The Dialogue of St. Catherine of Siena*, page 67, Loc. 1487, 1906.

245 By the way guys, just because Eve is the one that is featured in the story, men shouldn't think that they weren't there. We were there. Where else would we have been? Down at the bar watching the game? No, there was no bar to go to, no game to watch. Would we have been out running? No. Why would we have been exercising if we were in Eden with perfect health? Does anyone run just for the fun of it? No. Adam was right there beside Eve (Gen. 3:6), and his failure was that he didn't speak up; he didn't protect his wife from committing the sin. He just sat there and silently let his wife make that her own decision alone. He acquiesced in it. So as much as I hate to say it, we men are not out of the loop here.

246 From Gen 3:1-5. [Emphasis added.]

I believe that the root of sin is when we decide we want to reject God's will in our life, and we want to be in control. Sinning is in effect making ourselves into god: taking control of our lives, our destiny. It is telling the true God, "No, I reject your divinity. I am my own god, making my own rules, setting my own destiny."

If we reject God, we reject reality. Think about that for a moment. You and I really create nothing. We may manipulate created things into a form that did not exist before, but we really don't create anything, bringing something out of absolutely nothing. Only God can really create. So if we reject God, we are necessarily rejecting reality. If we choose ourselves, we are choosing a fantasy, an illusion, just smoke and mirrors. As Psalm 81 tells us, turning from God leads to catastrophe:

"But my people did not listen to my words;
Israel would not submit to me.
So I thrust them away to the hardness of their heart;
'Let them walk in their own machinations.'" [247]

As St. Alphonsus Liguori says in his book *The Practice of the Love of Jesus Christ*, "We must ... love God as it pleases God, not as it pleases us." [248] It doesn't matter that we don't like or even understand God's way. After all, He is God, and we are not.

Although this wording of the First Commandment is pretty imperious, alternative wordings (which are as valid) clearly connect this Commandment to holiness as selfless love. We are told to love God and put aside all of our idols. If you think about it, all idols are about getting what we want, selfish love. And

---

247 Psalm 81: 12-13.
248 St. Alphonsus Liguori, *The Practice of the Love of Jesus Christ*, Chapter XIV, Section 17, page 163, translated by Peter Heinegg (Liguori Publications, 1953) p. 125. Hereinafter, the *"Practice."*

idols are all around us. The First Commandment is about loving God above all other things, selflessly.

The Second Commandment [249]

"You Shall Not Take the Name of the Lord Your God in Vain."

When God appeared to Moses on Mount Horeb, Moses asked for His Name. When "they ask me, 'What is his name?' what do I tell them? God replied to Moses: I am who I am. Then he added: This is what you will tell the Israelites: I AM has sent me to you." [250] At that time, God revealed His name to Moses, and in the ancient world, that was significant.

The Jews held the proper name of God in high regard. In order to avoid using it, the Jews came up with other ways to refer to Him: El Shaddai; Elohim; and Adonai are just a few examples.

At the opposite extreme is contemporary American society. We banter the word "God" around like we would "cat" or "dog." One of the common phrases you hear or see in emails and texts is "OMG." People don't think anything of it. When something (almost anything) happens, you'll hear people say, "Oh my God!" This can be used as an expression of joy, of surprise, or of disgust – almost anything.

We also regularly hear God's name in hellish curses. They can either be directed at a particular person or just as an indirect expression. If you think about that, what a horrible thing it is to ask God to send someone to Hell.

I was once driving with a priest friend, and someone cut us off.

---

249 CCC ¶ 2142-2167
250 Ex. 3:13-14.

Instead of cursing at the guy or insulting him (which was a bad habit of mine), I said, "Well, blessed be God!" The priest looked at me confused for a moment and then asked, "What's wrong with you?"

If we really love someone, we won't want to say anything bad about them, even when we are angry or frustrated with them. We will want to respect them. In the case of God, we will want to show Him reverence given who He is. Using His name only respectfully is one way of showing Him that we love Him. And holiness is all about love.

The Third Commandment [251]

"Remember the Sabbath Day,

To Keep It Holy"

There are certain passages in scripture that are particularly frightening to me. One of them is found in Luke 13:22-30.[252] Jesus is explaining that although the road to Hell is wide, the door to salvation is narrow. Some will knock trying to get in, protesting that they ate and drank with Him and that He taught in their streets, but He will say to them, "I do not know where [you] are from. Depart from me, all you evildoers!"[253]

Jesus spent his entire ministry preparing and building His Church.[254] One of the very first things that He did was to choose His Apostles.[255] He sent them to proclaim the Kingdom.[256] He

251 CCC ¶ 2168-2188.
252 See also Matt. 7:13-14.
253 Luke 13:27.
254 CCC ¶765.
255 Luke 6:12-16; Matt. 10:1-4; and Mark 3:13-19.
256 Matt. 10:7.

gave them the power to forgive sins.[257] He instituted the Eucharist and told the Twelve to repeat it in His memory.[258] When Jesus ascended into Heaven, He did not leave us as orphans.[259] He gave life to the Church by sending His Holy Spirit.[260] He charged the Apostles with the mission of the Church: "Go, therefore, and make disciples of all nations.... And behold, I am with you always, until the end of the age." [261]

After His death and resurrection, the Apostles continued what Jesus had taught them. John went to Ephesus. Thomas went to India. Mark (though close to Jesus, he was not one of the Twelve) went to Alexandria, Egypt. Peter and Paul went to Rome. They all went to spread the gospel.

Around 55 A.D., St. Paul wrote about how he received from Jesus the tradition of the Eucharist.[262] In about the year 105, on his way to Rome to be thrown to the lions in the Colosseum, St. Ignatius of Antioch (†108) wrote that, "I am the wheat of God, and am ground by the teeth of the wild beasts, that I may be found the pure bread of Christ." [263] Traditionally, this has been understood as a reference to the Eucharist. As I mentioned earlier, in about the year 155, St. Justin Martyr wrote a letter explaining how prayers are said over bread and wine, and that the bread and wine are transformed into the flesh and blood of Jesus. [264]

If we really want to grow closer to God and be a part of the body

---

257 John 20:23.
258 Luke 22:19 and 1 Cor. 11:23-26.
259 John 14:18.
260 Acts 2:1-13; John 20:32.
261 Matt. 28:19-20.
262 1 Cor. 11:23-26.
263 Ignatius of Antioch, Letter to the Romans, Chapter 4, ¶1.
264 First Apology, 66.

of Christ, frequent reception of the Eucharist would be assumed. For Catholics, we keep the Lord's Day holy by going to Mass.

Regularly attending Mass reinforces in us God's view of reality; and that is truly the only reality. We are constantly bombarded by the world's view of reality through TV, radio, movies, newspapers, magazines ... in fact, every kind of media that surrounds us. And it is constant. Everywhere we turn, the noise is blasting at us a message of self-love and self-empowerment. We need an antidote to that, and we find it at Mass where passages of the Bible are read to us, and the priest or deacon explains to us the truths of our faith and our true relationship with God. Where else will we hear the truth? Going to Mass gives us the chance to understand reality for what it truly is.

I think it may be necessary here to say something about the scandals that have recently hit the Church. One of the reasons that people give for leaving or rejecting the Catholic Church is the sins of the ministers or the hypocrisy of the faithful. Admittedly, these are real problems, but they are missing the point. Jesus should be our focus. I think that a story from the life of St. Francis of Assisi illustrates the point.

Towards the end of his life, at the age of 44, St. Francis was very frail. He had spent years fasting. He spent many sleepless nights in prayer. In the end, he needed the help of his brothers to travel at all.

One day, he was passing by a village with some of his brothers. When the villagers found out that St. Francis was passing by, they went to meet him and implore him to come to their village. They took him to the rectory where the parish priest was living with his girlfriend (a not uncommon practice at the time). When the priest came to the door, he was probably chagrined to see St. Francis.

The villagers proceeded to accuse the priest of his immoral behavior. They certainly expected St. Francis to condemn the man.

Instead, St. Francis fell to his knees, took the priest's hands in his own stigmatized hands, kissed them, and said, "All I know, and all I want to know, is that these hands give me Jesus."

As the story of St. Francis shows, the Church is about Jesus, not the clergy.

In 1809, Napoleon's troops kidnapped Pope Pius VII for refusing to bow to Napoleon's demands. Napoleon couldn't understand the Vatican's refusal to follow his orders. He supposedly said, "Don't you understand that I can crush the Catholic Church?" At which Cardinal Consalvi, the Vatican Secretary of State, calmly responded, "If in 1800 years we clergy have failed to destroy the Church, do you really think that you'll be able to do it?"

Throughout its history, the Church has survived turmoil and even scandal. God will bring us through anything that we are facing now. In fact, God always brings great good out of evil, so it will be exciting to see what He will do next.

If we focus on the sins of the ministers or of the laity, we are entirely missing the point. Jesus is the point. Jesus is the sole reason for our Church.

If we reject the Church, we are throwing back in God's face one of the greatest gifts He gave to us. We are telling God, "No, we are not interested." God doesn't give up on us, but I think a part of us dies whenever we do this.

Jesus makes Himself present to the world through his Church. Guided by the Holy Spirit, the leaders of the Church compiled, and the Church continues to preserve the Bible down through the centuries. It is the Catholic Church that is God's primary means of proclaiming the Gospel and sanctifying the world. It is only through the Church that we receive sanctifying grace, a share in the very life of God, through the sacraments. In particular, it is only through the Catholic Church that we have the Mass by which Jesus Christ, body, blood, soul, and divinity, becomes truly present to the world. Keep holy the Sabbath, and we will be holy.

The Fourth Commandment [265]

"Honor Your Father and Your Mother,
That Your Days May Be Long in the Land Which
the Lord Your God Gives You."

With the Fourth Commandment, we turn to the Commandments that deal with the love of others. It is no coincidence I think that the first of these focuses on the family.

Although the Fourth Commandment is couched in terms of the duties children owe to their parents, the Church understands it in a broader sense. It governs the whole family dynamic, and since the family is the fundamental building block of society, it impacts society as a whole.

The family is the primary, fundamental unit of any society. In a sense, it is primordial. Ideally the family is not only where children are raised and cared for, but it is also where children learn their moral values through the mutual self-giving of the parents

---

265 CCC ¶ 2197-2157.

to one another, of the parents to the children, and even between and among the children. As the basis of society, the family is a privileged community prior to anything else in the general society[266] and should be respected by every public governing authority which not only has a duty to recognize and respect it, but also to foster it.[267]

We need to keep in mind that in creating men and women and blessing the institution of marriage for the good of the spouses and for the generation and education of children,[268] God has shown us that the natural family is the normal reference point by which the different forms of family relationships should be evaluated.[269] And it is through the lens of the family (as properly understood) that all other societal relationships should be viewed.[270]

If the family is, in fact, the basic, the primary, unit of society from which all other relationships spring, it is important to look at those intra-family duties. And it seems that since parents normally feel a natural obligation to their children, the Fourth Commandment focuses on the duties of children to their parents.

I would think that most people would want to live by this Commandment more than almost any other. It is the only Commandment with a promise. In our society, people are always trying something new so we can live just a little while longer. According to God, the solution is simple: honor your mother and father, and you will live long.

---

266 CCC ¶2202.
267 CCC ¶¶2209-11.
268 CCC ¶2249.
269 CCC ¶2202.
270 CCC ¶2212.

Yet so many times we fail to do this. People, of course, are imperfect. Many of our parents - no, all of our parents - were imperfect to a greater or lesser degree. Some of us have deep wounds from things they said or did, and I don't mean to minimize those.

But God calls us beyond our hurts and our pains. He calls us to healing and forgiveness. God's medicine is very odd too: it is through forgiveness that we are healed. Resentment about things that were done or said to or about us is like a festering wound that can become a deadly infection. Forgiveness is the cure.[271]

This duty of honoring our parents is really fundamental considering what they did for us:

With your whole heart honor your father;
your mother's birth pangs do not forget.

Remember, of these parents you were born;
what can you give them for all they gave you?[272]

So how do we honor our mother and father? My dad used to always say, "If you can't say something nice, just don't say it." So don't run down your parents when talking about them.

In Sirach it also says,

My son, be steadfast in honoring your father;
do not grieve him as long as he lives.

Even if his mind fails, be considerate of him;
do not revile him because you are in your prime.

---

271 A beautiful example of this is Immaculee Ilibagiza who after hiding in a bathroom for 3 months with 7 other women during the Rwandan genocide found it in her heart personally to forgive the man who had brutally killed her family. See *Left to Tell: Discovering God Amidst the Rwandan Holocaust*, by Immaculee Ilibagiza, Hay House 2003.

272 Sir. 7: 27-28.

*Kindness to a father will
not be forgotten;
it will serve as a sin offering
— it will take lasting root.*[273]

So if your parents are older, make a real effort to visit them. Human interaction is huge. When they become frail, don't just warehouse them in a nursing home. If possible, bring them into your own home.[274] If that isn't possible, make a real effort to

*First Saturdays
Our Lady of Fatima promised
consolation and assistance at the
time of death to anyone who (with
the intention of making repara-
tions for our ingratitude) on the
first Saturdays of 5 consecutive
months (1) goes to confession
(reconciliation), (2) receives Holy
Communion, (3) recites the Rosary, and (4) keeps Mary company
for 15 minutes while reflecting
on the mysteries of the Rosary.*

visit them or to stay in touch often. During their lifetimes (or even after their deaths), you could observe the five First Saturdays as Our Lady of Fatima requested, offering it up for them. Our Lady promised the graces necessary for salvation for those who offer this devotion. And after your parents have died, pray for them every day. Include them in every one of your Mass intentions. Also, we can pray the Stations of the Cross, while offering it for a plenary indulgence for them.

We can look at this Commandment in this way: selfless love begins at home with loving our parents. Holiness begins at home.

The Fifth Commandment [275]

"You Shall Not Kill "

It would be nice to say that this commandment which prohib-

---

273 Sir. 3:12-14.
274 See Matthew 25:35-36.
275 CCC ¶¶ 2258-2330.

its something so cruel, so horrible, is not an issue for us, but that would not be true.

Several years ago, a friend asked me if I would engage in a debate about abortion with the president of the Missouri chapter of NARAL (the "National Abortion and Reproductive Rights Action League"). The moderator knew that I was passionately opposed to abortion, but he also knew that I could civilly discuss the topic.

I only wanted to ask two basic questions: 1) "When does human life begin?" and 2) "Why do you take that position?" It seems to me that if we say human life begins at any time other than conception, we have to defend some very troubling euthanasia situations. A week before the debate, the NARAL president backed out.

Over 3,500 babies are aborted in the US daily. Since *Roe v. Wade* was decided, approximately 60 million babies have been killed.

One study indicated that the vast majority of abortions in the US are a personal choice: the baby is ill-timed; I/we already have enough children; the baby would be an economic burden. Abortion is more convenient than having the baby.

To me, this is reminiscent of the child sacrifices that were practiced in the Old Testament. In those days, children were sacrificed to the demon Moloch to win favors such as more wealth, better crops, an easier lifestyle, that sort of thing. I am reminded of a comment attributed to Mother Teresa: "It is a poverty to decide that a child must die so that you may live as you wish."

In addition to the abortion issue, we are going to have to face the growing push for assisted suicide. The marketing line I am hearing regarding this is "death with dignity." The motivating force is that we want to relieve people of their suffering. Yet,

that can be allayed with better and more effective pain manage-
ment - not death. It seems to me that the indignities and incon-
venience that surround death are more of a problem for those
who are not dying. It seems that if we were more supportive of
the dying by offering better love and concern, as well attending
to their physical suffering, they could truly die naturally with
true dignity.

Many feel that the death penalty also runs afoul of this Commandment. And, basically, it does. That's why Pope Francis has
revised the text of the Catechism regarding the death penalty.
However, a close analysis of what was and was not revised con-
firms what Cardinal Dulles once wrote: "[t]he magisterium does
not, and never has, advocated unqualified abolition of the death
penalty." [276] Still, Pope Saint John II noted that, "as a result of
steady improvements in the organization of the penal system,
such cases [calling for the death penalty] are very rare, if not
practically non-existent." [277]

My personal thought is that if we assume that a prisoner has
committed a capital crime, then he or she has committed a mortal sin. If they die in the state of mortal sin, they will go to Hell
(subject to the miraculous mercy of God). If we allow the prisoner time to repent, they could avoid Hell. Yes, they might have to
spend a considerable amount of time in Purgatory, but we can
look at Purgatory as the vestibule of Heaven. If we make it there,
we will end up in Heaven. And God wants us all to be saved. But
that is just my personal position.

---

276 Avery Cardinal Dulles, *Catholicism and Capital Punishment*, First Things (April 2001), www.firstthings.com/
     article/2001/04/catholicism-capital-punishment, p. 5.
277 John Paul II, Evangelium Vitae, §56.

And it isn't enough just to sit on the sidelines. Silence is complicity.

The sanctity of human life – all human life – is rooted in the fact that humans are created in the image and likeness of God.[278] "Endowed with 'a spiritual and immortal' soul, the human person is 'the only creature on earth that God has willed for its own sake.'"[279] To intentionally destroy innocent human life, to kill another human being without some just cause, is an offence against both the dignity of the human being and the holiness of God. In a very fundamental way, it is a horrendous act of blasphemy.

The Sixth[280] And Ninth[281] Commandments

"You Shall Not Commit Adultery"

"You Shall Not Covet Your Neighbor's Wife"

The act of conceiving a child is sacred. At no other time in our lives do we ever participate in an act of creation. When a man and woman come together and conceive a child, they are by the grace and power of God *cooperating* with Him in the creation of a new person, a new human being. Yes, we combine already existing genetic material, but more than that, those cells are "*en-souled.*" In cooperation with God, we participate in creating a new human being, someone who was not there before the marital act.

How can that not be holy? How can that not be sacred?

Whether it is sex outside of marriage, masturbation, pornog-

---

278 CCC ¶1700.
279 CCC ¶1703, quoting from Gaudium et Spes, 14 §2, and 24 §3.
280 CCC ¶¶ 2331-2400.
281 CCC ¶¶ 2514-2533.

raphy, sterile sex (that is, birth control or homosexual acts), or any other abusive sex, we are taking something that is fundamentally sacred and using it for our own selfish purposes and not how God intended it to be used.

In addition, profane sex is an assault against another person. Even if it is consensual, it is profane: we're just using the other person (perhaps mutually) as an object to satisfy our desires. We are taking what is holy and using it as common, secular. In a very real sense, it is dehumanizing. Instead of loving another human being, we are objectifying them, demeaning them.

In the case of homosexual sex, we often hear as an excuse that the person was born that way, so how could it be wrong? But as I mentioned in discussing relativism, we don't have the right to just decide for ourselves what is right and wrong. If we did, then there would be no absolutes. Taking that reasoning to its ultimate end, society could (and at times has historically) justify the most heinous of actions.

Just because people in our fallen nature have an inclination to do something, that does not in and of itself make it right. God is calling us to something more than that.

Pope St. John Paul II wrote extensively on the sacredness of the fundamentally humanizing act of marital love in *The Theology of the Body: Human Love in the Divine Plan*. Christopher West has taken John Paul's deep reflections and simplified them for the rest of us to understand.[282] Taking the time to read what has been written on this subject would seem to be invaluable to me, particularly since our society has so twisted our understanding of sex.

---

282 Christopher West, *The Theology of the Body Explained: A Commentary on John Paul II's "Gospel of the Body,"* Pauline Books & Media (2003).

St. Paul emphasizes this point in his first letter to the Corinthians.[283] He reminds his readers that we are not our own. We are temples of the Holy Spirit. He says that since we have been purchased at such a great price, we should glorify God in our bodies.[284]

We live in a super saturated sexual society. Everywhere we turn, there is sex: TV, magazines, billboards, movies, and our music. And the depiction of sex is exploitative. The images depict sex as a way to gratify our own desires. It is not about the other person. It is just about satisfying lust.

The problem with all of these images is that they all affect us. Studies have shown that viewing pornography chemically affects the brain. Sexual imagery seems to imprint on the brain much faster than other imagery. Maybe more than other sins, pornography can become addictive and result in the destruction of relationships, particularly a marriage. It can destroy families; it creates unreasonable expectations of sexual intimacy; and in our society, pornography seems to be everywhere.

We need to be on guard about downplaying the power of sexual exploitation. I've heard a number of people (particularly guys) say, "You can look at the menu, so long as you don't order. You can order, so long as you don't eat. You can eat...." Well, you get the idea.

Jesus said:

> "You have heard that it was said, 'You shall not commit adultery.' But I say to you, everyone who looks at a woman with lust has already committed adultery with her in his heart." [285]

---

283 1 Cor. 6:15-20

284 1 Cor. 6:19-20.

285 Matthew 5:27-28.

St. Dominic Savio (†1857) lived in Turin, Italy, in the mid-1800s. He was one of the boys who worked with St. John Bosco (†1888) (whom we will consider later). When St. Dominic walked down the street in public he would keep his eyes to the ground. He did not want to view anything that would stir up lust. Jesus was even more emphatic. Speaking hyperbolically, of course, He said that if your eye causes you to sin, you should pluck it out.[286] In speaking to Jacinta, one of the children at Fatima, Mary warned us of the gravity of sexual sin. She said that more souls would go to Hell for the sins of the flesh than for any other.[287] That should be sobering for us all. We do not take this as seriously as we should in our society. The problem with sin is that it takes something beautiful and life-giving, and turns it into something dark and destructive. We should glory in God's creation.

And how does this promote holiness? Profane sex is using people as objects to satisfy our own selfish desires. Chastity both in and outside of marriage respects the dignity of the other person in a selflessly loving way.

And since I am writing this Handbook particularly for the laity, I want to end this part with a word about marriage.

As I mentioned earlier, holiness is all about selfless love. But our society is consumed with a plague of self-love that is infecting even marriage. Many people marry just for what they can get out of the other person; and when they have what they want and there is nothing more to take, they get a divorce.

Catholic marriage is not like that. St. Paul talks about marriage in the fifth chapter of his letter to the Ephesians.

---

286 Matt. 5:29. He was not encouraging self-mutilation. He was strongly emphasizing His point for the spiritual development of His followers using a manner of speaking that was common in His time.
287 Apostoli, *Fatima for Today*, op. cit., Kindle p. 145, 244.

"He who loves his wife loves himself. For no one hates his own flesh but rather nourishes and cherishes it, even as Christ does the church, because we are members of his body. 'For this reason a man shall leave [his] father and [his] mother and be joined to his wife, and the two shall become one flesh.'" [288]

When he says that wives should be subordinate to their husbands,[289] his comments upset some people, and they stop listening. What they ignore is that this reflection begins with the statement that both spouses should be subordinate to one another.[290] And he goes on to say that husbands should love their wives as Jesus loved His Church.[291] To understand this last comment, we need to remember that for the love of the Church, Jesus died on the Cross. Husbands are called to give up their lives for their wives, and that is the root of holiness in marriage: dying to ourselves for love of the other. In doing that, we are imitating Christ, becoming Christ to our spouses and our families.

The Seventh[292] and Tenth[293] Commandments

"You Shall Not Steal"

"You Shall Not Covet ... Anything That Is Your Neighbor's."

All praise to God who in creation has provided for us everything that we need, even in a superabundance. If managed properly, He has provided what everyone needs to live comfortably. Eco-

---

288 Eph. 5:28-31, quoting Gen. 2:24.
289 Eph. 5:22.
290 Eph. 5:21.
291 Eph. 5:29-30.
292 CCC ¶¶ 2401-2463.
293 CCC ¶¶ 2534-2557.

nomic life, properly understood, is the well-ordered balance of people owning and making use of things for the good of all mankind[294] and of workers putting into effect the gifts and talents received from God for the glory of God.[295] God is truly good.

But we live in a consumer based society. In one way or another, we produce things and then try to get people to buy what we produce. The products we make may address a certain need or we may produce something and then try to *manufacture* a "need" for it. And even if there is a real need, we will probably produce more of that thing than we really need, and then we will try to inflate that real need into a greater perceived need. The more things we sell, the more money we will make.

Once the marketing people convince us that we "need" something, we gradually begin to think that we have a right to that thing. If we have a need, then there must be a corresponding right to it. So we think we are entitled. And if we are entitled, then we begin to envy the people who have the things that we believe that we are entitled to. Envy is a sadness about what other people have and our immoderate desire to possess those things.[296]

As history shows, and as we know from our own lives, envy of what other people have can lead to the worst crimes.[297] Cain killed Abel out of envy.[298] In the First book of Kings, we hear the story of how the evil queen Jezebel killed Naboth to get his vineyard for her husband, King Ahab.[299] And even in our own day, many people steal out of envy: that person has what I want,

---

294 CCC ¶2402.
295 CCC ¶2427.
296 CCC ¶ 2539.
297 CCC ¶ 2538.
298 Gen. 4:1-8.
299 1 Kings 21:1-16.

what I "need." And in certainly the most extreme situation, we have heard that some women have killed pregnant women to steal the baby out of the mother's womb. Envy can lead to truly horrible crimes.

Coveting is envy, the desire to possess or to have something. The Tenth Commandment tells us that we shouldn't covet what other people have. This Commandment stands in stark opposition to envy. It forbids greed and the desire to amass earthly goods without limit.[300] It should come as no surprise in our society, where most people have more than they really need, we experience so much theft. We intentionally create an envy of what other people have and that leads to a sense of entitlement based on a perceived need. People steal because of a real or perceived need.

The Seventh Commandment prohibits theft. When someone steals from us, we are offended. It's an affront to our human dignity. We feel that we have a right to own things, and the Seventh Commandment implies that. The Catechism tells us that "the earth is divided up among men to assure the security of their lives.... The appropriation of property is legitimate for guaranteeing the freedom and dignity of persons and for helping each of them to meet his basic needs...."[301] We have a right to own things, and stealing what belongs to others is wrong.

But the right to private ownership is not absolute. The law of charity clearly supersedes the right to private ownership. Jesus encouraged a perhaps radical view of property ownership. Jesus

---

300 CCC ¶ 2536.
301 CCC ¶ 2402.

tells us that we should seek the Kingdom of God first.[302] He tells us that we cannot be His disciple unless we renounce everything that we have.[303] He tells us that we should sell what we have and give to [the] poor.[304] When the rich man who tried to obey all of the Commandments asked what more he could do, Jesus said, "If you wish to be perfect, go, sell what you have and give to the poor..." [305] In the Gospel of Luke, Jesus praises Zacchaeus when he pledges to restore four-fold anything that he has stolen.[306] And several of the Saints have done the same.

When crowds went out to be baptized by John the Baptist, he called them to repentance. When they asked him what they should do, he said, "Whoever has two tunics should share with the person who has none. And whoever has food should do likewise." [307]

In one of his sermons, St. Basil the Great said that if a man owned two cloaks but only needed one, he was stealing from the poor. In another sermon, he said,

> *"Do you not see how people throw away their wealth on theatrical performances, boxing contests, mimes, and fights between men and wild animals, which are sickening to see, and all for the sake of a fleeting honor and popular applause? If you are miserly with your money, how can you expect any similar honor? Your reward for the right use of things of this world will be everlasting glory, a crown of righteousness, and the kingdom of heaven; God will welcome you, the Angels will praise you, all men who existed since the world began will call you blessed." [308]*

302 Matt. 6:33; and Luke 12:22-31.
303 Luke 14:33
304 Luke 12:33.
305 Matt. 19:21; Mark 10:21; and Luke 18:22.
306 Luke 19:9-10.
307 Luke 3:11.
308 *Homily on Charity*, 3, 6: pp. 31, 267, 275. (Office of Readings, 17th Week of Ordinary Time.)

The early church is held up to us as a model for sharing things in common.[309] We are told how Barnabas sold a piece of property and put the money at the feet of the Apostles.[310] And religious communities almost universally are based on common ownership of everything, creating a mutual dependency. The Catechism points out that, "Abandonment to the providence of the Father in heaven frees us from anxiety about tomorrow." [311]

Yes, things are necessary. We need to eat. We need a safe place to sleep and to provide shelter from the weather. And we need clothing for warmth and for modesty. But things should not be the sole or even the primary focuses of our lives. The ownership of property is not the problem per se. It is how we use the gifts that God has given to us.

According to the Catechism, "In the beginning God entrusted the earth and its resources to the common stewardship of mankind..." [312] The Catechism refers to this as the "universal destination of goods." [313] "The goods of creation are destined for the whole human race." [314] We are just the stewards of the earth's resources.

When we think of the economy, we often imagine a tension, if not an actual conflict, between those who own property and other resources and those who work, those who provide the labor. This is how Marx viewed economics.

As Catholics, we understand that the economy is meant to be a cooperative effort. Each group has both rights and duties: the owner has the right to own his or her property, but also the duty

---

309 Acts 4:32-35.
310 Acts 4:36-37.
311 CCC ¶2547, citing to Matt. 6:25-34.
312 CCC ¶ 2402.
313 CCC ¶ 2403.
314 CCC ¶ 2402.

to use property for the good of themselves but also for the good of others; the laborers have the right to be able to provide for their family, but also the duty to work to the best of their ability for the glory of God and to provide for their family. As Pope Pius XI wrote in his encyclical *Quadragesimo Anno,*

> *Therefore, with all our strength and effort we must strive that... the abundant fruits of production will accrue equitably to those who are rich and will be distributed in ample sufficiency among the workers - not that these may become remiss in work, for a man is born to labor as the bird to fly - but that they may increase their property by thrift, that they may bear, by wise management of this increase in property, the burdens of family life with greater ease and security, and that, emerging from the insecure lot in life in whose uncertainties non-owning workers are cast, they may be able not only to endure the vicissitudes of earthly existence but have also assurance that when their lives are ended they will provide in some measure for those they leave behind.*

The Seventh Commandment has something of a panoramic scope: the poor must respect the rights of the rich, but the rich must respect and foster the dignity of the poor as persons created in the image and likeness of God. And the Tenth Commandment is like a guide to how we do that: do not place inordinate value on things.

I think it is fair to say that we have a lot of injustice in our society, so we have a lot of work to do. We need to keep in mind that our Lord said, "[t]he measure with which you measure will in return be measured out to you." [315] Selfless love (holiness) dictates that we respect other people's property while at the same time providing for the legitimate needs of others.

---

315 Luke 6:38.

The Eighth Commandment[316]

"You Shall Not Bear False Witness Against Your Neighbor."

I once had to get an order signed by a judge. When I got to the courtroom, there was a hearing in progress. I listened to the two opposing expert witnesses testify about some financial issue. I thought they both sounded reasonable, although they reached entirely different conclusions.

When the hearing was over, I went to meet with the judge in his chambers. I told him that I thought he would have a tough time deciding between the two competing arguments. He said it wasn't that tough. When I asked him why, he simply said, "It's easy. They all lie."

They all lie? I was really caught off guard by that statement. Admittedly I was a bit naive, and the judge was kind of jaded, but it was still shocking to hear him just trash all of the testimony.

From my perspective as a lawyer, people bearing false witness strikes at the very heart of our society. In order to function, we need to be able to rely on what people tell us, especially about other people.

But it seems that bearing false witness has become common-place in our society. Slander is the making of a false statement with the intent to harm someone, and libel is the same but in written form. The slander and libel in our society is so prevalent that it is epidemic. Character assassination in politics now is *de rigeur*. Truth is often just an uncomfortable footnote.

The connection between this Commandment and selfless love, or holiness, also seems to be evident. The only reason

---

316 CCC ¶¶ 2401-2463

that we would lie about something someone said or did would be to get something for ourselves, often at another's expense. Being charitably honest about another person is clearly a way to love selflessly.

In reflecting on sin and the Ten Commandments, it is tempting to look at how other people have violated them and turn away from our own faults and failings. It is easier to judge others than to judge ourselves. But Jesus warns us about this. He says, "Judge not, that you not be judged." [317] Although we must always discern between what is good and what is evil, we should not judge the intentions and dispositions of other people.

One of my favorite stories in the Bible is the story in the eighth chapter of the Gospel of John of the woman caught in adultery.[318] In the story, the scribes and Pharisees bring a woman to Jesus who had been caught in the act of adultery. Citing Mosaic Law, they want Jesus to condemn her to be stoned. Jesus knelt down and wrote in the dust. When they continued to press Him, He said "Let the one among you who is without sin be the first to throw a stone at her." [319] At that, all of the accusers went away one by one. When the woman was left alone, He looked up and asked "Woman, where are they? Has no one condemned you?" When she said that no one had, He said, "Neither do I condemn you." [320]

No one knows what Jesus wrote in the dust. Some of the Church Fathers have speculated that He was writing out the sins of the accusers. When He said, "Let him who is without sin cast the

---

317 Matt. 7:1–5.
318 John 8:1–11.
319 John 8:7.
320 John 8:11.

first stone," all of the accusers would have seen that He already knew their sins. Since He knew, none of them could cast that first stone.

God knows all of our sins. We should be sufficiently aware of our own sinfulness to know that we should not cast that first stone either. It is my hope that in reflecting on the Ten Commandments, we are compelled to stop judging others and to grow in holiness.

The Ten Commandments correspond to Jesus' command that we love God above all things and our neighbors as ourselves. Although they can come off as legalistic – a set of mandatory rules – they are actually all about true, selfless love. And selfless love is what holiness is all about. "Love one another as I love you." [321]

I would be remiss if I didn't add one more thing in this discussion. We will fail. We are human. But Jesus through His Church has given us the solution: the Sacrament of Confession, or reconciliation. Aside from the mere psychological benefit of talking to someone about our failings, the miracle of the Sacrament is that Jesus empowered His priests to actually forgive our sins.[322] What a profound grace that is! We shouldn't pass it up.

"Be holy because I [am] holy."[323]

Works of Mercy

In the Our Father, Jesus tells us to pray, "Thy Kingdom come, Thy Will be done, on earth as it is in Heaven." Early in her history, the Church sought to provide guidance to the faithful about following the example of Christ and how to make this a reality.

---

321 John 15:12; cf. John 13:34.
322 John 20:23 and Matt. 16:19.
323 1 Peter 1:16.

In his letter to the Ephesians, St. Paul told the Christians there that they had to give up their old ways of darkness and alienation from God and live in righteousness and holiness.[324] Following the advice of St. Paul, the Church has encouraged Christians to pray and practice penance, but also to strive, by works of mercy, to put off the "old" man and to put on the "new."

Over time, the Church developed the fourteen works of mercy: seven corporal and seven spiritual. All of them are rooted in scripture either directly or indirectly. Jesus told us that we will be judged by whether we perform acts of mercy[325] or fail to do so.[326]

One of the early Church Fathers, Origen (†254), said, "He 'prays without ceasing' who unites prayer to works and good works to prayer. Only in this way can we consider realizable the principle of praying without ceasing." [327] In more recent times, Pope St. John Paul II wrote that,

> *"Jesus Christ taught that man not only receives and experiences the mercy of God, but that he is also called 'to practice mercy' towards others: 'Blessed are the merciful, for they shall obtain mercy.' [Matt. 5:7.] The Church sees in these words a call to action, and she tries to practice mercy."* [328]

We have to live our faith.

God is all about mercy.[329] After the Israelites had worshipped the golden calf and Moses had destroyed the first set of tablets with the Ten Commandments on them, he went back up the

---

324 Eph. 4:17-24.
325 Matt. 25:34, 40.
326 Matt. 25:41, 45.
327 Quoted at CCC ¶2745.
328 Pope Saint John Paul II, *Dives in Misericordia*, ¶14.
329 Of course, God is also a God of justice. Sin has consequences and is not treated the same as virtue – not in the Old Testament and not in the New Testament. But the first thing we should think about when we think of God is mercy.

mountain for God to replace the tablets. When he was there, God revealed Himself to him, passing before him and proclaiming, "The LORD, the LORD, a God gracious and merciful, slow to anger and abounding in love and fidelity, continuing his love for a thousand generations, and forgiving wickedness, rebellion, and sin...." [330] In his letter to the Ephesians, St. Paul tells us that "... God ... is rich in mercy, because of the great love he had for us...." [331] In the Book of Wisdom, it says, "But you have mercy on all, because you can do all things; and you overlook sins for the sake of repentance." [332] Jesus told us that God desires mercy more than sacrifice: "Go and learn the meaning of the words, 'I desire mercy, not sacrifice.'" [333] Peter tells us that God wants everyone to be saved and for none to perish: "[God] is patient with you, not wishing that any should perish but that all should come to repentance." [334]

One of Jesus' most memorable parables is the Parable of the Prodigal Son. After the son wasted all of his premature inheritance, he returned to the father. The son comes to his father to confess his guilt and ask only for a job. His brother was indignant and resentful. The father, on the other hand, was overjoyed that his son had returned. All the past was forgiven and forgotten. The father felt nothing but love and mercy for his son, as God does for us. The father cannot restrain his joy. [335]

We are told there is vast joy in Heaven over the repentance of each sinner. [336] As the Catechism points out, the entire Gospel

---

330 Ex. 34:6-7.
331 Eph. 2:4.
332 Wis. 11:23.
333 Matt. 9:13; see also Matt. 12:7; Mark 2:17; cf. 1 Tim 1:15.
334 2 Pet. 3:9.
335 Luke 15:11-24.
336 Luke 15:7.

is the revelation in Jesus Christ of God's mercy to sinners.[337] Although God is perfectly just, God has revealed that He is profoundly merciful.

I want to turn now to the positive aspects of holiness: the "do's" if you will. These are the actions that all of us should strive to perform, to put love for our neighbor into action. I am going to look at these "do's" through the Works of Mercy. They are basically taken from the Bible.

In the 25th Chapter of Matthew, Jesus talks about the last judgment:

"When the Son of Man comes in his glory, and all the angels with him, he will sit upon his glorious throne, and all the nations will be assembled before him. And he will separate them one from another, as a shepherd separates the sheep from the goats. He will place the sheep on his right and the goats on his left. Then the king will say to those on his right, 'Come, you who are blessed by my Father. Inherit the kingdom prepared for you from the foundation of the world. For I was hungry and you gave me food, I was thirsty and you gave me drink, a stranger and you welcomed me, naked and you clothed me, ill and you cared for me, in prison and you visited me.' Then the righteous will answer him and say, 'Lord, when did we see you hungry and feed you, or thirsty and give you drink? When did we see you a stranger and welcome you, or naked and clothe you? When did we see you ill or in prison, and visit you?' And the king will say to them in reply, 'Amen, I say to you, whatever you did for one of these least brothers of mine, you did for me.' Then he will say to those on his left, 'Depart from me, you accursed, into the eternal fire prepared for the devil and his angels. For I was hungry and you gave me no food, I was

---

337 CCC ¶ 1846.

thirsty and you gave me no drink, a stranger and you gave me no wel-
come, naked and you gave me no clothing, ill and in prison, and you
did not care for me.' Then they will answer and say, 'Lord, when did
we see you hungry or thirsty or a stranger or naked or ill or in prison,
and not minister to your needs?' He will answer them, 'Amen, I say to
you, what you did not do for one of these least ones, you did not do
for me.' And these will go off to eternal punishment, but the righteous
to eternal life." [338]

What Jesus is saying here is that we will be judged by what we
do. In the letter of St. James, he points out rather emphatically
that faith without works is dead. [339]

In discussing the corporal (or physical) works of mercy and
the spiritual works of mercy, it should be enough simply to list
them, but that just becomes an academic exercise. I decided it
would be better to illustrate them using the lives of Saints to the
extent possible.

This approach created a selection problem. All of the Saints ex-
hibit many of these Works of Mercy. It is sometimes hard to say
that a particular Saint's life reflected one virtue more than another. And then there is the problem of which Saint to pick.

So in going through the Works of Mercy, I picked some of my favorite Saints to illustrate a particular virtue. Could I have picked
another Saint for any given virtue? Absolutely! Could the Saint
I have chosen for any one of the virtues have been chosen just
as appropriately to illustrate another virtue? Again, absolutely!

So in reflecting on how the Saints have lived out a particular
virtue, feel free to substitute your favorite Saint. Or do some re-

---

338 Matt. 25:31-46.
339 James 2:14-26.

search and find another Saint for that virtue. Since the Saints are our heroes, it's all good.

Corporal Works of Mercy

I once heard that there is an old adage among missionaries: we can't preach the gospel to someone who is cold and hungry. It is almost an imperative that we first tend to people's physical needs.

The first seven Works of Mercy are referred to as "corporal" or bodily. They are physical actions with regard to the physical needs of people. It is important to note that these are not just

The Corporal Works of Mercy:
1. *Feed the Hungry*
2. *Give Drink to the Thirsty*
3. *Clothe the Naked*
4. *Shelter the Homeless*
5. *Visit the Sick*
6. *Visit the Imprisoned*
7. *Bury the Dead*

acts of social work. A person doing just social work is doing an act of kindness, but we are talking about something more than that.

Misplaced or distorted kindness can justify a lot of evil things. Some might say it would be unkind to bring a possibly handicapped child into the world or to bring a child into a less than perfect situation; or it would be an act of kindness to euthanize an old person when they are no longer able to live a "full" life or when they are suffering from dementia; or it would be an act of kindness to help someone commit suicide when they are facing a difficult and painful death. Mere kindness does not provide a moral compass.

The southern Catholic writer Flannery O'Connor once observed:

> *"In the absence of ... faith now, we govern by tenderness. It is a ten-derness which, long cut off from the person of Christ, is wrapped in*

theory. When tenderness is detached from the source of tenderness, its logical outcome is terror. It ends in forced-labor camps and in the fumes of the gas chamber." [340]

We are called to something more than mere tenderness. St. Rose of Lima (†1617) would bring the poor and sick into her own home to care for them. This annoyed her mother who reproached her for it. St. Rose told her mother, "When we serve the poor and the sick, we serve Jesus. We must not fail to help our neighbors, because in them we serve Jesus." [341] More recently, Mother Teresa (†1997) used to say the same thing. When people asked her how she could so lovingly care for all of the sick and dying people she picked up out of the street, she said it was easy because she was caring for Jesus.

Along the same lines, Dorothy Day (†1980) (the great Catholic social activist of the 20th century) once said, "The mystery of the poor is this: That they are Jesus, and what you do to them you do for him. It is the only way we have of knowing and believing in our love." [342]

And St. Teresa of Avila once noted that:

"Christ has no body on earth now but yours, no hands but yours, no feet but yours. Yours are the eyes through which the compassion of Christ must look out on the world. Yours are the feet with which He is to go about doing good. Yours are the hands with which He is to bless His people."

340 Flannery O'Connor, *Mystery and Manners: Occasional Prose*, Farrar, Straus and Giroux; 1 edition (January 1, 1969)

341 CCC ¶ 2449.

342 *Dorothy Day Selected Writings*, Robert Ellsberg, Ed. © 1983, 1992, 2005 by Robert Ellsberg & Tamar Hennessey, Orbis Books, Maryknoll, NY.

As the Apostle John wrote, we cannot love the God we do not see if we don't love the brother or sister we do see.[343]

Fr. Thomas Dubay in his book, *Fire Within*, contrasted social activism with Christian charity: "[T]he mystic is identified with the expansive and the universal, but the mere activist is restricted in focus, constrained by the limiting and the particular."[344] And Mother Teresa once wrote, "… without our suffering, our work would just be social work, very good and helpful, but it would not be the work of Jesus Christ, not part of the redemption."[345] In other words, the social activist is focused on a particular need of an individual, whereas Christian charity looks more broadly at the whole person and his or her eternal well-being.

The moral compass of acts of mercy is more than mere kindness. It is more than just a set of perhaps arbitrary and mutable rules or nice sayings. It is a person: Jesus Christ. It is all about loving God through loving our neighbors.

Many of these corporal works of mercy can be accomplished by working with your local St. Vincent de Paul Society. They visit the homebound, provide food and clothing where needed, help with heating bills when possible, and even help with yard-work. Actively participating in the Society is a great way to exercise the corporal works of mercy.

Feed the Hungry[346]

This is an easy to understand work of mercy. We can prepare a meal at a homeless shelter. We can work at or contribute to a food pantry. For parents, just feeding our ravenous children is a work of mercy.

---

343 1 John 4:20.
344 *Fire Within*, Loc. 6205, by Fr. Thomas Dubay, S.M., Ignatius Press (1990).
345 Mother Teresa in a letter to her sisters dated the First Friday of July, 1961, quoted from *Come Be My Light*.
346 Matt. 14:15-21, 25:35; Luke 3:11, 9:12-17; John 6:35; Proverbs 22:9; Isaiah 58:10; and 2 Kings 4:42-44.

St. Elizabeth of Hungary (†1231) was born in 1207. Her family was local royalty, and at a very young age, for political reasons, she was promised as the wife of the young son (Louis) of a neighboring noble. She and Louis were married when she was 14. Although this marriage was for political reasons, it seems to have been a happy and very loving one. Both Elizabeth and Louis were devout Catholics.

Elizabeth was always looking out for the poor. She built a hospital at the base of the family castle to care for the poor who became ill. Daily she would visit them to comfort them personally. She would also feed the poor. She would take bread from the castle, bundle it up in her cloak, and carry it through the streets to distribute.

Although Louis supported this ministry, many of those in the court resented Elizabeth. She made them look bad. So they started spreading rumors that Elizabeth was stealing treasure from the castle. Once when she was taking bread to the poor, Louis ran into her when he was returning from hunting. Under pressure from the nobles, Louis asked her to open her cloak to show them what she had. When she obediently opened her cloak, red and white roses were all anyone could see.

St. Elizabeth of Hungary, pray for us that we may
always be willing to share with the poor and the hungry
the blessings that God has given to us.

Give Drink to the Thirsty [347]

The slave trade was a horrible business. People would capture African natives and sell them to the traders. They would be

---

347 Matt. 10:42, 25:35; Isaiah 55:1; and Rev. 21:6, 22:17.

herded (like cattle) into the hold of a ship. They were chained and severely confined during the ocean passage. They were given little to eat or drink. There were no sanitary facilities, so they basically would live in their excrement. Disease and even death were very common. It was inhuman.

Although 16th and 17th century travel from western Africa to the eastern American seaboard could take 7 to 14 days depending on the wind and the weather, Lima, Peru, is on the western side of South America. In good weather and with favorable winds, the passage would take three weeks or longer, as ships had to go around Cape Horn at the southern tip of South America. The slaves that arrived at Lima would have been confined much longer than their North American-bound counterparts. And they would have been in much worse shape because of that. But at least during part of the 17th century, Martin de Porres would have been there to greet them.

St. Martin de Porres (†1639) was the illegitimate son of a Spanish gentleman and a freed slave from what is now Panama. His father abandoned them early, so Martin grew up in deep poverty. After only two years of formal education, he was apprenticed to a barber, a surgeon (yes, the barbers were the surgeons then), and he learned the medicine of the time.

When he was 15, he applied for admission to the Dominicans. Because of his mixed-race heritage, he could only be admitted as a servant to perform menial tasks. However, because of his character and intelligence, he was put in charge of handling the distribution of aid to the poor. Then, after eight years in the Order, the prior permitted Martin to take his formal vows, although some of the members of the community continued to mock him for his being a bastard and for his mixed race heritage. Because of his training as a surgeon, when he was 24, he was put in charge of the infirmary where he stayed the rest of his life. And miracles abounded.

Perhaps because of his heritage, Martin had tremendous compassion for the Africans who arrived in Lima on board the slave ships; and there were many of them. Peru imported more slaves than America. Whenever a ship arrived, Martin and one or two other Dominicans would rush to the harbor and perform a kind of triage, separating the dying from the sick and the sick from the healthy. With the merely sick, he would treat them with the herbs and the medical treatments of the day. With the dying, he would comfort them, just giving them a drink of clean water after the burning heat of the ship's filthy hold.

We know that there are many more "saints" – those blessed, though unacclaimed, souls who loved God and their neighbor with their whole hearts. Maybe all that they did was to provide something as simple as a refreshing drink of water to someone with a parched throat. But we know that this is blessed act of mercy because Jesus Himself said, "Anyone who gives you a cup of water to drink because you belong to Christ, amen, I say to you, will surely not lose his reward." [348] And there is no better authority than that.

St. Martin de Porres, pray for us that we will always be
willing to share even the little things that we have to provide
at least some small comfort to those in need.

Clothe the Naked[349]

A friend of ours established a little charity to provide, among other things, a coat to school children in the inner city. It turned

---

348 Mark 9:41; Matt. 10:42.
349 Matt. 25:36.

out that many of them slept in unheated homes, and they had to sleep in their coats. Needless to say, their coats began to smell, and the other children kept away from them. Our friend decided to provide them with a second coat to wear during the day. There are many little charities like that. Something as simple as that meant a lot to those children. We can do this kind of work through a clothing drive.

St. Martin of Tours (†397) lived in the 4th century. During his lifetime, the official Roman persecution of Christians stopped, and Christianity became legal, though it did not become the official religion of the Empire until 380.

Martin is beloved for a number of reasons, but one of them has to do with clothing a naked beggar. Martin's father was a Roman tribune, a high-ranking officer in the Imperial Horse Guard. It was expected that Martin would follow suit. When Martin was only ten, much to his parents' displeasure, he attended a Catholic Mass and became a catechumen. However, he wasn't baptized for some time (not an uncommon thing in those days), and at fifteen, he was required to join the cavalry like his father. At age 18, he was assigned to a division that appears to have been the emperor's bodyguard. Once, early in his service and before he was baptized, he was in the city of Amiens when he encountered a naked beggar. Since it was cold, Martin took off his own cloak, cut it in half with his sword, and gave half of it to the beggar. That night Martin had a dream in which Christ appeared to him and said, "Martin, a mere catechumen, has clothed me."

St. Martin of Tours, pray for us that we will respond to Christ's call to clothe the naked as if we were clothing Christ Himself.

Shelter the Homeless[350]

This may be one of the most organized works of mercy around. There are any number of shelters around, and yet it seems that we still have an enormous homeless problem. One way that we can help is by volunteering at or contributing to a homeless shelter. I have a particular affinity to homes for unwed mothers and families, but everyone deserves a roof over their heads. An interesting characteristic of the Benedictines is that because of the Rule of St. Benedict, they always provide hospitality (both food and shelter) for travelers as well as for the poor.

When Americans think about the French Revolution, they often compare it to the American Revolution. That is so wrong. The better comparison would be the Communist Revolution. In France, faithful Catholics, religious, priests, and bishops were marched onto galley slave ships and left to die of starvation and disease while the ships just sat in the harbors. Some, like the Discalced Carmelite nuns in Compiegne, were marched to the guillotine (the good sisters singing hymns of praise to God on the way) and beheaded. The French Revolution devastated French civilization and opened the door to Napoleon and his wars. France in the early 1800s was a tattered society.

St. Jeanne Jugan (†1879) was born in the midst of the French Revolution. She saw the havoc wracked on her small town in northwestern France. She saw how the events around her were crushing the poorest of the poor, particularly the old widows whose husbands had died in the tumultuous times. So she took them in – first into her own home (even giving up her own bed

---

350 Matt. 25:35.

and sleeping in the attic) – and then in an abandoned convent. Some other local, generous young women were moved by her compassion and joined her. And the poor elderly kept coming. Soon the ministry spread across France. Her ministry grew into an order, the Little Sisters of the Poor, and continued to spread to England, Belgium, Spain, Ireland, and eventually to North America. To this day, the almost 2,400 Little Sisters provide shelter and care for the poor elderly in 234 houses around the world. For information, including vocation information, please go to www.littlesistersofthepoor.org.

> *St. Jeanne Jugan, inspire us to provide for those who*
> *(like our Lord) have nowhere to lay their heads.*

Visit the Sick[351]

This work of mercy may be something as simple as visiting someone who is homebound. It tremendously brightens their day. We can also take someone to a doctor's appointment when they would have great difficulty making it there themselves. It might mean sitting with them as a doctor gives them a devastating diagnosis. Or it could mean distributing communion at a hospital or nursing home. In all of these, you are visiting the sick.

St. John of God (†1550) lived in what is now Portugal in the early 1500's. He started life as a shepherd, but when his employer tried to force him to marry his daughter, John fled and joined the army. We don't know many details of John's life in the military, but he must have had a really "good" time because after the age of 40, he deeply regretted his behavior, and he turned to Catholicism.

---

351 Matt. 25:36.

John was a very impetuous person. Once, after his conversion, he encountered some Franciscans heading to Morocco to offer themselves in exchange for the Christians who had been kidnapped by the Muslims, and almost without thinking, he was off to Morocco. When a priest in Morocco told him he was needed more back in Spain, off he went. When he saw books and pamphlets being printed on the newly invented printing press, he

The Franciscans are a religious order founded by St. Francis of Assisi (†1226), following Christ by living in poverty to unite themselves more closely to the mission of Christ here on earth and to reach out to the poor and forgotten in the world.

started selling religious works on the streets basically at cost. For a while he inflicted such severe penances on himself that the townspeople thought he was insane, and they had him locked away. St. John of Avila (†1569), a great preacher, visited him and convinced him to moderate his penances. After that, he found his true calling.

At the time, there were many poor ill people who had no one to care for them or anywhere to go. When John would see these people, his heart ached. He started taking them into his home and caring for them. After a while, he was able to rent a large place to house more of the sick. He would beg in the streets during the day, and care for the sick at night. He spent everything he had on the destitute. He would borrow money from people he knew, but there was never enough money for everything, so he could not pay back what he borrowed. In one of his surviving letters, he talks about how he was afraid to go outside of the house at one point for fear that his creditors would seize him and throw him in jail for his unpaid debts.[352]

He also would risk his own life for the people he was caring for. One time, when there was a fire in a hospital and everyone was just standing around watching it burn, he rushed in and either carried or led the patients out. When all of the patients were out, he went back in to get the blankets, bedding, and mattresses. The civil authorities brought in a cannon to blast one part of the building to save the rest. John stopped them, went onto the roof, and with an ax separated the buildings, but in the process he fell through the burning roof. Although everyone thought he was dead, he miraculously walked out of the burning remnants.

By age fifty-five (55) he had almost totally spent himself in his service to the sick. Yet when he heard that a flood was bringing much needed driftwood near his town, he went down to the river to retrieve the wood to keep his guests warm. When one of his young companions fell in the river in the process, without a thought for himself, John jumped in to save the boy, but caught pneumonia as a result. He died soon afterwards.

St. John of God, patron of the sick, pray for us.

Visit the Imprisoned[353]

This is one of the tougher works of mercy in my mind. Very few of us want to go to a prison to visit. But there are ministries out there that do that very thing. We can sup-

Kairos Prison Ministry is a faith-based ministry that addresses the spiritual need of imprisoned men, women, youth, their families, and all who work with them. Check to see if there is a local chapter you can help, and if not, investigate starting one.

---

352 Office of Readings, Saint John of God, March 8, Second Reading.
353 Matt. 25:36

port them in one way or another. We can support them financial-
ly and with our prayers. We can contribute books for the prisoners to read; we can provide any support possible to those who are
going into the prisons. And helping those released from prison to
re-enter society should be included in this work of mercy.

Northern Italy in the 1800's had a lot of problems. In the early years of the century, Napoleon went marching through on
his way to Rome to imprison Pope Pius VII. Along the way, he
laid waste to the cities, towns, and villages he passed through.
Through all of this, there was a radical displacement, and in some
cases impoverishment, of many people. Many young boys were
abandoned on the streets of the cities to fend for themselves. And
many of them turned to crime. Turin, Italy, was no exception.

Joseph Cafasso (†1860) was born in 1811 in a small town in
northern Italy. He was born with a deformed spine. He was small
and weak, but very devout. Early in his life he decided to become
a priest. He did well in the seminary and continued studies after
ordination. He became a famous professor in moral theology,
and at a fairly young age, he was appointed as the superior of
the seminary college. He often helped poor students with books,
and when necessary, even money.

In addition to his academic work, Fr. Cafasso had a special
concern for prisoners. He would go to the prisons and spend
hours hearing confessions, providing counsel, and helping
however he could. He got the nickname of the "Priest of the Gallows" because he attended (as a friend and priest, and not in
any official capacity) 68 executions. He would hear their confessions, encourage them, listen, stay with them through the night
before their execution, and even ride with them in the cart to

the gallows. He offered personal penances and mortifications for them, praying long hours before the Blessed Sacrament that none of them would be lost to Hell. His work with prisoners inspired Servant of God Juliette Colbert (†1864) to work among the female prisoners.

St. Joseph was canonized in 1947.

> *St. Joseph Cafasso, comfort of prisoners and*
> *those condemned to die, pray for us.*

Bury the Dead[354]

In my work as an estate planning attorney, I go to a lot of funerals. Some of my kids have told me that I have the most depressing job in the world since I deal with so much death and dying.

Normally funerals have family and friends that gather from all over. There is a wake the night before. At least here in St. Louis, we seem to have developed a custom of putting up a display of pictures of the decedent, and everyone talks about what a nice person he or she was. At the funeral, the priest will usually say some kind words, and after the Mass, there is often a eulogy by a friend or family member that does the same kind of thing.

I once attended a funeral that had none of that. The decedent's only sister had died a couple of years earlier. There were no children or nieces or nephews. The woman had been perhaps a little cantankerous, so there was only one neighbor couple, our parish mourners, some trust officers, and me at the funeral. This started me thinking about what we really are doing at funerals.

Some may think that burying the dead is an odd act of mercy

---

354 Tobit 1:17-19.

since the person is dead. They may see it as a necessity for health reasons. They may see it as a way to wrap things up for the survivors. Many think that we should just cremate the body and dispose of the ashes in some convenient way.

It is interesting to remember that the practice of burying the dead is an ancient custom in many societies. Archaeologists are constantly finding the graves of ancient communities. And most of them contain artifacts that were buried with the deceased. Maybe the Egyptian pyramids are the best examples of this. But why bury things with a dead person? Surely they won't need them.

I think that things were buried with the dead and their bodies were treated with such great respect precisely because these ancient societies thought the deceased would need them. Communities that buried the dead with great respect had a strong belief in the afterlife, and some thought that the deceased would need their bodies in that afterlife.

It is interesting to note that in Hinduism, cremation is the norm. They do not believe in the resurrection of the body but a sort of migration of the soul through "reincarnation." The soul simply moves to another physical body. Hindus cremate precisely because they do not believe in the resurrection of the body. The soul is not necessarily a part of the body in their religion.[355]

We see at the time of Christ a sort of mixed understanding of the resurrection of the dead. Although the Pharisees believed in the resurrection, the Sadducees did not. However, even Jewish scripture reports that burying the dead was an action of mercy.[356]

---

355 Of course, it should be noted that the Catholic Church permits cremation, provided that it does not demonstrate a denial of the resurrection of the body. In addition, the cremated remains must be buried. See CCC ¶2301 and Code of Canon Law 1176.3.

356 Tobit 1:16-20.

As Catholics, we believe that the body and soul are fundamentally entwined. As the Catechism teaches us:

> *The unity of soul and body is so profound that one has to consider the soul to be the "form" of the body: i.e., it is because of its spiritual soul that the body made of matter becomes a living, human body; spirit and matter, in man, are not two natures united, but rather their union forms a single nature.*[357]

We are a body-soul composite. Our practice of burying the dead reflects our belief in the resurrection of the body. And our belief in the resurrection of our bodies is directly tied into our belief in Christ's Resurrection. As St. Paul points out in his first letter to the Corinthians, to deny the resurrection of our bodies is to deny the Resurrection of Christ.[358] To deny the Resurrection of Christ is to deny our very faith in Christ.

Respect for and burying the body of a deceased person is a statement of our own faith in the Resurrection. Preparing a person's body for burial is an act of charity since we are preparing the body for the final resurrection.[359] The purpose of a funeral is really two-fold: to comfort those left behind; and to commend the deceased to the mercy of God. Jesus consoled Martha and Mary on the death and loss of Lazarus, and we should console one another on the passing of a loved one. But for Catholics who believe in Purgatory, we are also at the funeral to pray for the repose of the soul of the decedent. We are praying that God will have mercy on their soul and will quickly admit them into Heaven. We are praying for a short stay (or maybe even no stay)

---

357 CCC ¶365, referencing the Council of Vienne (1312).
358 1 Cor. 15:13.
359 CCC ¶ 2300.

in Purgatory. This is precisely why burying the dead is an Act of Mercy. We are consoling those left behind and preparing our friends and loved ones for the Resurrection and helping them on their way to Heaven.

> *Dear Father, give us the charity to treat the mortal*
> *remains of the deceased with the respect due to them in our*
> *sure and certain hope of the resurrection and to*
> *pray for Your mercy on them.*

Spiritual Works of Mercy

We live in a world full of suffering. Yes there is physical suffering, but I wonder if the spiritual suffering is even worse. I remember reading that Mother Teresa once said that the biggest disease in our world today is not a sickness, but it is rather the feeling of being unwanted, uncared for, and deserted and abandoned by everyone.

The Spiritual Works of Mercy:
1. *Counsel the Doubtful*
2. *Instruct the Ignorant*
3. *Admonish Sinners*
4. *Comfort the Afflicted*
5. *Forgive Offenses*
6. *Patiently Bear Wrongs*
7. *Pray for the Living and the Dead*

We see it all the time. We see people who are confused and disillusioned. Marriages end in painful divorces. Children are neglected or abused. People are used for what someone can get from them, and not treated with the dignity that human beings deserve. And psychologists tell us that although we live in the age of the cellphone when everyone seems to be connected to everyone else all of the time, loneliness is on the rise – dramatically so. There is a lot of spiritual suffering in the world.

We all understand the corporal works of mercy. They are acts of caring motivated by our love of God and of our neighbors because of Him. The spiritual works of mercy are a little more esoteric. They address the spiritual needs that we all have. Although they may not be as readily apparent as the physical needs of people, they are just as critical to us as human beings.

Before getting started looking at each one of these, it might be helpful to note that the first three spiritual works of mercy may be a little tricky. How do we charitably admonish the sinner? How do we get people to open up about their doubts? How do we instruct the ignorant without sounding condescending? These must all be approached with deference and tact, but they shouldn't be ignored. They just need to be approached carefully. The remaining spiritual works of mercy are much more approachable. So let us begin.

Counsel the Doubtful[360]

This work of mercy calls on us to provide people with gentle, Christian guidance in their faith journey. We have to be careful not to come off as being preachy or lecturing.

The Gospel was first preached in Japan in the early 1500's thanks to the work of St. Francis Xavier (†1552). By the end of that century, it is estimated that there were around 300,000 souls who had entered the Church out of a population of maybe 8,000,000.

This large number of conversions made several groups in Japanese society very uncomfortable. It posed a threat to the established religious communities; the traditional Japanese saw it as a threat to their traditional society; and then there are always

---

360 Matt. 13:18-23; Mark 4:13-20, 9:14-29; Luke 8:11-15; and John 14:27.

the sinners who don't want to be converted. Needless to say, the large number of people converting to Catholicism created tremendous tensions in Japanese society.

In addition, there was a political dimension. The Japanese were fearful of being invaded by European powers. They did not want to be taken over by Westerners, and so any foreign influence was suspect. When in the mid-1590's a Spanish ship bound for Japan was captured off the Japanese coast, it was discovered that the ship was carrying artillery. Chaos ensued.

The discovery of the artillery set off a sort of panic in Japan. Westerners were expelled. The government began an intense and cruel persecution of any native Japanese citizen suspected of sympathies with the Europeans, including Catholics. Twenty-six prominent Catholics were rounded up and sentenced to death – by crucifixion and lancing. They were forced to march 600 miles to Nagasaki. They were publicly tortured to terrorize other Japanese Catholics. But they all bore their sufferings courageously, singing the Latin hymn of praise, the "Te Deum," when they arrived at the hill of their martyrdom.

Among the 26 martyrs was a Japanese priest by the name of Fr. Paul Miki (†1597). All along the march, he had preached to the crowds, encouraging the faithful to persevere in their faith. In mockery of the Cross of Christ, these martyrs were crucified. Even from his cross, he sought to encourage the believers, preaching a sermon from his last "pulpit."

When Christian missionaries were again allowed into Japan in the 1860s, at first they found no trace of Christianity. But after establishing themselves, they discovered thousands of Christians who had preserved the faith privately in their homes. I be-

lieve in large part that was due to the example and encouragement of Paul Miki and his companions who are now recognized
as Saints in the Church.

St. Paul Miki, please pray for us that we may encourage the doubtful
even when it is inconvenient or even risky for us.

Instruct the Ignorant[361]

It goes without saying that no one wants to be lectured. However, parents fulfill this work of mercy by bringing their children
up in the Catholic faith, talking to them about what it means to
live our faith in a secular world. It also includes Catholic education, whether at grade school, high school, or colleges and uni-
versities. It can include working in our parish catechesis or RCIA
programs. Finally, it can include lovingly correcting someone's
misunderstanding of the faith or of Catholic history.

As I mentioned earlier in discussing sheltering the homeless,
the French Revolution devastated French civilization. In the
small towns across France, many devout parents were killed,
leaving orphans everywhere. Cold and starving, these children
struggled to survive, much less to grow in their faith.

Julie Billiart (†1816) was born in 1751. At 22, someone attempt-
ed to kill her father. It shocked her so much that she lost the use
of her legs. Over the next 22 years, her health continued to dete-
riorate as the paralysis spread to more parts of her body, even to
the point of affecting her ability to speak clearly.

When the French Revolution broke out, Julie's faith was steadfast. In her small town, everyone thought of her as a holy woman
who continued to praise God even through her suffering. The

---

361 Matt. 28:19-20; Mark 16:14-18; Luke 24:47-49; John 20:21; and 2 Tim. 3:16-17, 4:1-5.

local apostate "priest" who had sworn allegiance to the French Revolution and government went to visit her to convince her to sign the oath of allegiance as an example for everyone else in the village. Not only did Julie send him away, but she started telling everyone not to receive sacraments from him. When the government spies found out, they sent soldiers to arrest Julie. Her friends smuggled her out of town in a cart covering her with hay.

Julie spent several years in hiding thanks to her friends, moving from town to town, staying just ahead of the government agents. In each town she visited, she saw destitute children, the heirs of the French Revolution. Her heart was moved with pity. Yes, she was concerned about their physical poverty, but more than that, she was concerned about their salvation. She was particularly concerned about the young girls who had few opportunities to provide for themselves, much less for any children they might have. Without education, the girls couldn't learn their faith, and they certainly couldn't pass it on to their children.

From these concerns grew the Sisters of Notre Dame de Namur. The primary stated purpose of the Sisters was, and to this day is, the salvation of poor girls using education not as an end, but as a means to help them and their children to get to Heaven. It must surely have been God's will that Julie do this work because as soon as the Order began, through the prayers of a local priest, Julie was completely healed of her paralysis so that she could without impediment devote all of her energies to that work for the rest of her life.

St. Julie Billiart was canonized by Pope Saint Paul VI in 1969.

St. Julie, pray that we may see what is blocking
the path to Heaven in ourselves and in those around us

and that in charity and only by the grace of God we
may work to remove those obstacles so that we may all
one day rejoice with you and all the saints in Heaven.

Admonish Sinners[362]

Hell is a horrible place, and it is forever. So it is a supreme act of love and mercy to try to help others understand that certain acts or omissions are truly, if not even profoundly, sinful. It is merciful to try and help them to avoid even the near occasion of sin. The problem is that some people resent interference, and some even really like their sins.

The circumstance may arise where we can actually talk to someone about something they are doing without causing a major battle. Although those battles may not go anywhere, there are times when they are necessary. There are other times when we need to preach by our actions; we simply live our faith. Decline an invitation to go to a bar where you know that temptations will be great. Don't go to explicit movies with friends. Decline to read a book you know is inappropriate. And avoid those parties where you are pretty certain sinful things will occur or grave temptations will be present. Sometimes, actions speak louder than words.

John Bosco (†1888) was born in a small community in northern Italy. His father died when he was two, leaving him and his two older brothers to help their devout mother when they were old enough to work the farm. There was little time and even less money for an education. When a family friend gave John a book to read, one of his older brothers became angry. He felt betrayed

---

362 Luke 15:7, 17:3; 2 Tim. 4:2; and Proverbs 27:17.

and turned on John making his life at home very difficult.

When John was around nine years old, he had his first dream, one of many for which he would later become famous. In it, he saw his future vocation as a priest.

About that time, he also saw a magic show. The show amazed him, but the crowd that gathered gave him an idea. He learned magic tricks and began performing for the neighbors. At the end of the show, he would repeat the sermon he had heard earlier that day at Mass and invite his audience to pray with him.

At twelve, he left home to find work to earn money to send home to support his family. Soon afterwards a priest befriended him and gave him enough education to enter the seminary, including teaching him Latin. After his ordination, his first assignment was Turin.

In order to help street urchins from ending up in prison (and worse, in Hell), John began what eventually became the "Oratorio." He rounded up the boys from the factories and the streets. On Sundays, they had to go to Mass, but he also organized outings and appropriate entertainment for them. He felt that wasn't enough, so he started a trade school system. In order to keep the boys from falling under bad influences, he also tried to provide them housing. Housing them in his own home at first didn't work so well since they would steal the blankets in the house and the hay from the barn. He looked for alternative arrangements and established a dormitory in the slums. They had to relocate several times because the neighbors were a little nervous having that many street urchins living right next to them.

The boys were a pretty rough lot, growing up poor, abandoned, and desperate. John followed the counsel of St. Francis de Sales and disdained corporal punishment, but he was stern with the boys in other ways. He continuously admonished the boys to avoid sin. In his dreams, he would see the threats the boys faced in regard to their salvation, and the fear of losing any one of them to Hell broke his heart. St. John spent the rest of his life battling for the souls of the children, both through his advice and through his prayers.

> *St. John Bosco, please pray that we will know what to say to charitably admonish sinners in our lives so that we can all gain Heaven, the only thing that really matters.*

Comfort the Afflicted[363]

To comfort a person in need is one of the greatest acts of mercy imaginable. This involves taking time to be with people who are suffering from an illness, a loss, or just from the burdens of life. I think that a lot of times, the comfort we can provide is just listening with a kind and sympathetic heart. We are just trying to comfort their troubled souls.

Alfred Bessette (†1937)[364] (one of my favorite Saints) was born in 1845 in the northern part of the Canadian province of Quebec. His health was so bad that Alfred was baptized right after birth for fear that he would die. His health continued to be an issue for the rest of his life.

Alfred's father was a carpenter. In those days, carpenters couldn't go down to the lumber yard for their wood. Instead, they had to cut down trees themselves and prepare the wood. When Alfred was nine, his father was on the wrong side of a tree

---

363 Matt 11:28-30; John 14: 27, 16:22-23; 1 Pet. 5:5-11; Rev. 21:4; Psalms 9:8-11, 22:23-27, 27:4-5, 30:2-4, 46:2, 55:22, 56, 71:20-22, 116, 119:49-50; Jer. 29:11-14; Lamentations 3:21-24, 31-33; and Nahum 1:7-8.
364 Biographical information is taken from Jean-Guy Dubuc, *Brother Andre: Friend of the Suffering, Apostle of Saint Joseph*, Ave Maria Press (2010).

when it fell, and he died. Then, when Alfred was twelve, his beloved, saintly mother died of tuberculosis. He and his siblings
were orphans.

Alfred was shipped between relatives and worked at various
jobs, but no one could find anything he was particularly good at.
Finally, a priest met Alfred and saw great potential in him. He
strongly recommended Alfred to the Holy Cross fathers at a high
school in Montreal saying that he wasn't sending them a postu-
lant, "I'm sending you a saint."

Alfred took the name of Andre when he entered the Holy Cross
community. After the initial year, the community decided to
send Andre away because of his poor health. Throwing himself
at the feet of the visiting local archbishop, Andre pleaded to be
allowed to stay and be admitted to the order. The archbishop
replied by saying that anyone who wanted to be admitted that
badly surely should be allowed to join.

But there was the problem of what to do with Brother Andre.
He really wasn't very good at much. Because he was orphaned so
young and had been shipped between family members, he was
basically illiterate. The Holy Cross community decided to make
him the porter, the person who would answer the door, greet
visitors, and find whoever they had come to see. Andre was also
assigned various other menial chores like sweeping and mop-
ping the floors.

One day when he was sweeping the floor in the school infirmary, there was a boy lying in bed. As Brother Andre walked past
him, he asked the boy what he was doing. The boy told him that
he was sick, and that he was told to lie there. Brother Andre told
him he was not sick, and that he should go out to play. The boy

insisted that he was sick, and Brother Andre insisted he was not. The boy suddenly realized that he was feeling better, much better. He got up, got dressed, and went out to play. When one of the teachers saw him, he yelled at him to go back to the infirmary. The boy told him that Brother Andre had told him to go out and play. He hustled the boy back to the infirmary. While the doctor was examining the boy, he gave Brother Andre a sharp talking to. But the doctor concluded that the boy was perfectly healthy now, although he had been very ill before. That was the first healing for Brother Andre.

As time passed, people began to realize that Brother Andre was a great person to turn to when they were troubled, much like other holy porters the Church has had in her history such as St. Alphonsus Rodriguez (†1617), Conrad of Parzham (†1894), and Blessed Fr. Solanus Casey (†1957). Visitors would come with their troubles, and Br. Andre would offer advice. In addition, he would pray for them and would sometimes anoint them with oil from the votive lamp that hung in the high school chapel in front of the altar of St. Joseph (to whom Br. Andre was greatly devoted). Miracles followed. To this day, the back wall of the Oratory of St. Joseph in Montreal is lined with many of the crutches, braces, and other medical apparati that people left behind after being cured.

Br. Andre may have learned compassion from all of the troubles he had suffered in his life. His love and inspired wisdom were evident to all the souls who sought him out, and in one way or another, he comforted them. Brother Andre was canonized in 2010 by Pope Benedict XVI.

St. Andre Bessette, pray that we may always find the time to just listen to the troubles of others and to offer comfort when we can.

Forgive Offenses[365]

People get righteously indignant over the slightest things: someone cuts in front of us in the checkout line or on the highway; someone takes the last piece of pie or drinks the last cup of coffee; or someone gets acclaim for an accomplishment that was not theirs. However, it is critical to remember that in the Our Father, Jesus conditioned our own forgiveness on our forgiveness of others. And many spiritual directors will tell us that holding on to those offenses is like leaving an infected wound untreated.

Immaculee Ilibagiza survived the Rwandan genocide where all but one of her family and many of her friends were brutally hacked to death. She found that the only way to go on with life after such a horror was to forgive. She tells her story in her book, *Left to Tell.*[366]

In the early years of the twentieth century, Maria Goretti was the young daughter of a poor farmer in Ferrier di Conca, Italy, south of Rome. One day when she was 12 and her family was working out in the field, Maria was mending clothes at home. The neighbors' son, Allesandro, approached her and tried to rape her (it apparently wasn't the first time he had tried). She protested saying that it was a sin. He became angry and choked her saying he would kill her if she didn't let him have his way. She said it was a mortal sin and that he would go to hell for it.

---

365 Matt. 6:14-15, 18:15-35; Mark 11:25; and Luke 11:4, 17:1-4.
366 Immaculee Ilibagiza, *Left to Tell*, op. cit.

When she continued to refuse, he took a knife and stabbed her 11 times. As she fled for her home, he stabbed her 3 more times. He tried to escape, but he was caught and put in jail.

Maria did not die immediately. She was taken to a local hospital. When the doctor heard the story and saw the extent of her injuries, he asked her to pray for him when she was in Heaven, and she agreed. The next day she forgave Allesandro and said that she wanted to have him in Heaven with her someday. Then she died.

Allesandro was convicted of the murder. He was originally going to be sentenced to life in prison, but because he was a minor (and also because he came from a family with a history of mental illness and alcoholism), the sentence was reduced to 30 years.

He remained unrepentant for three years in prison. At about that time, he had a dream. In the dream, Maria gave him lilies (a symbol of humility and devotion, but also innocence after death). When he took the flowers, they burned his hands. That was apparently the beginning of his repentance and conversion.

After his release from prison, he went to Maria's mother and asked for forgiveness. She said that if Maria could forgive him, how could she refuse? The next day they went to Mass together.

Allesandro soon entered a Capuchin monastery as a lay brother where he worked as a receptionist and a gardener until his death. He reportedly prayed every day to Maria and referred to her as "my little saint." He was present at her canonization Mass in 1950.

> *The Capuchins are a branch of the Franciscans. Their communities were formed to focus on solitude and penance in the spirit of St. Francis.*

St. Maria Goretti, pray for us that we will find it in our
hearts to forgive those who have hurt us in our lives,
no matter how deep the wound may be.

Patiently Bear Wrongs[367]

Even as children, we have a great sense of right and wrong. All of us feel that life should be fair. That sense of fairness seems to be born in us. We feel that we have our rights, but our sense of those rights is inevitably violated during a lived life. As Christians, we are asked to patiently bear all of the wrongs that we suffer, offering them up to God, submitting our will to His Will.

A good example of that is St. Pio of Pietrelcina, commonly known as Padre Pio. Padre Pio was a model monk. He prayed constantly, said Mass with tremendous reverence, and heard confessions for hours on end.

At different times in his life, God blessed him with certain graces. When he heard confessions, if you forgot a sin, he would remind you of it to make a full confession. When he was thirty-one, he received the gift of the stigmata, the blood of which sometimes smelled like perfume. He had the gift of healing. He would sometimes levitate during prayer. He could be in two places at the same time (bilocation). All of this caused a great stir among the people. All of the attention seemed to have embarrassed him.

But Padre Pio had his critics. There were several prom-

> *The stigmata is the physical appearance of the wounds of Christ in the body of a person. The first person to receive the stigmata was St. Francis. Since then, there have been a number of people who have receieved the wounds, many of them women.*

---

367 Matt. 5:38-48; Luke 6:27-36; and 1 Pet. 2:18-19.

inent people who claimed that he and his Capuchin brothers were faking it for financial profit. One physician and psychologist called Padre Pio "an ignorant and self-mutilating psychopath who exploited people's credulity." Even Pope Pius XI doubted the truth of the reports.

Beginning in 1921, Padre Pio was banned from saying Mass in public, hearing confessions, blessing people, answering letters, publicly showing his stigmata, or even communicating with his spiritual director. These sanctions continued for 10 years. Although we have to assume that this would have been devastating to him, we don't hear a word of complaint from Padre Pio or from those around him. He charitably submitted to all of this unfounded criticism, and much like Christ in His Passion, he did not open his mouth in protest. Eventually the ban was lifted, and Padre Pio was permitted to use these gifts for the greater good of the Church.

Padre Pio was canonized in 2002 as St. Pio of Pietrelcina, but people still refer to him affectionately as Padre Pio.

Padre Pio of Pietrelcina, pray for us that in imitation of Christ in His Passion we may lovingly bear the wrongs that God allows us to suffer for His own good purposes.

Pray for the Living and the Dead[368]

As I discussed above in regard to the burying the dead, we are called on to pray for one another, living and dead. Jesus expects that of us. It is a part of every Eucharistic Prayer at every Mass. It is a tremendous act of charity to ask for God's help for someone. No one can help more than God.

---

368 2 Maccabees 12:38-46.

St. Romuald (†1027) was born in Ravenna, Italy. His family was a member of the aristocracy. As a teenager, he apparently indulged in all of the vices that were common at that time to the nobility. That all changed when he was 20. His father was in a duel with a family member over some property. Romuald was his second. His father killed the opponent, and Romuald was horrified. He fled to a Benedictine monastery for a 40 day penitential retreat which became the basis for the rest of his life. At the end of the retreat, he applied for and was admitted to the monastery.

That didn't last long, though. His austerity was so severe that his fellow monks began to resent him. When the situation grew tense and he requested permission to leave, they readily granted his request.

For many years Romuald searched for his place in religious life. He would go to a monastery, stay for a few years as a hermit, and then move on. All the while his reputation grew. Eventually, he would be asked to go to problem monasteries and reform them, which he did. Romuald longed to be a martyr and was given permission to go to Hungary to preach, but every time he tried to preach, he would become terribly ill. He only recovered when he returned to Italy.

Finally he was given some land by a man by the name of Maldolus. It was there that the Ca'Maldoli hermitage was built, and a community of men gathered around him. This was the beginning of the Camaldolese Order. All of the brothers lived alone in their separate hermitages, coming together only for Mass, the Divine Office, and certain meals. Bread and water was the fare, and silence was the norm. It is not surprising that this way of life appealed only to a small number.

The purpose of monastic life is for the individual to grow in perfection. But Christianity is not an egocentric religion. An individual's path to perfection is necessarily intertwined with the salvation of all people. Since members of monastic orders try to get by on very little for themselves (especially the Camaldolese), they are not praying for themselves. They have dedicated their lives to praying for the salvation of the entire world, both the living and the dead. When a Camaldolese monk (or any other religious for that matter) prays, they are praying for all of us.

St. Romuald, pray for us and all of our loved ones, both
the living and the dead, that we may all join you one day in Heaven.

Virtue

Fundamentally, when we talk about holiness, we are talking about virtue. In her poem "On Virtue," Phyllis Wheatley (1753-1784) seeks to understand Virtue.

Oh thou bright jewel, in my aim I strive
To comprehend thee. Thine own words declare
Wisdom is higher than a fool can reach.
I cease to wonder, and no more attempt
Thine height t'explore or fathom thy profound.
But, O my soul, sink not into despair,
***Virtue** is near thee, and with gentle hand*
Would now embrace thee, hovers o'er thine head.
Fain would the heaven-born soul with her converse,
Then seek, then court her for promised bliss.
Auspicious Queen, thine heavenly pinions spread,
*And lead celestial **Chastity** along,*
Lo! Now her sacred retinue descends,

Arrayed in glory from the orbs above
*Attend me, **Virtue**, thro' my youthful years!*
O leave me not to the false joys of time!
But guide my steps to endless life and bliss.
***Greatness**, or **Goodness**, say what I shall call thee,*
To give me an higher appellation still,
Teach me a better strain, a nobler lay,
O thou, enthroned with Cherubs in the realms of day.

She begins by saying that Virtue is out of reach, unattainable. But she immediately says we should not despair because Virtue is, in fact, near to us. She comes to the understanding that Virtue is not attainable, except with God. To her, it is purity, goodness, and salvation.

It is to the Ten Commandments and the works of mercy that we turn first for virtue. But our search for "endless life and bliss" as Wheatley would have it, demands greater, more fulsome efforts.

It may sound easy: avoid evil and do good. But as I wrote earlier, sin is like an addictive drug. The more we sin, the harder it is to break those sinful habits. It's like stepping into quicksand: the more we fight it, the deeper we seem to get. That's like trying to fix things on our own without turning to God in trust and asking Him to save us. We really can't do that.

And our society sends us very confusing messages. We don't talk much about virtue in our self-indulgent society. We prize self-indulgence so that we can be all that we can be. But at the same time, in some cases, we do see incredible acts of charity and self-sacrifice. In a sense, every one of us has two faces, two aspects of our selves: a self-indulgent self and a self-sacrificing self. Our goal should be to overcome the self-indulgent self and to develop that self-sacrificing self.

In order to break those bad habits, we need to ask God for the grace to develop good habits. It's like asking God for a rope to help drag us out of the quicksand. The problem is that developing bad habits is amazingly easy. Developing good habits seems to be much harder. It's almost against our nature. That's concupiscence at work.

To develop good habits takes time, practice, and vigilance. And good habits develop into virtues. The more we practice virtue and develop those habits, and as those habits become dispositions, the more we become like Christ who personified and was the perfection of all virtues.

Virtues can be broken into two categories: human virtues and theological virtues. The Catechism tells us that: "Human virtues are firm attitudes, stable dispositions, habitual perfections of intellect and will that govern our actions, order our passions, and guide our conduct according to reason and faith." [369]

Based on classical philosophy, the Catechism identifies four principal **human virtues:**

Prudence: St. Thomas Aquinas defines it as "right reason in action." The Catechism goes on to say that it "is the virtue that disposes practical reason to discern our true good in every circumstance and to choose the right means of achieving it.[370]

Justice: Justice "consists in the constant and firm will [of the faithful] to give [what is owed] ... to God and neighbor." [371] It disposes us to respect the rights of others and to establish a balance

---

369 CCC ¶1804.
370 CCC ¶1806.
371 CCC ¶1807.

or harmony that promotes equity with regard to persons and the common good. We hear a lot about justice in our society, but I don't think that we have a proper understanding of it. Justice for us seems to mean letting people do whatever they want without any objective idea of what is truly good. Justice in our society is rooted in our false freedom. That is not true justice.

Fortitude: Fortitude "ensures firmness in difficulties and constancy in pursuit of the good." [372] When the going gets tough, the tough get going kind of thing. Fortitude enables us to conquer fear, to bravely face trials and persecution, and even to face death. This is the virtue of martyrs.

Temperance: This is not a popular virtue today. Temperance "moderates the attractions of pleasure and provides a balance in the use of created goods." [373] This is self-mastery over instincts and desires. The world pulls us towards all kinds of things that in the end are going to hurt us, and temperance pulls us back to what will actually be good for us.

In addition to the human virtues, there are three **theological virtues:** faith, hope, and charity.

Faith: "Faith is the theological virtue by which we believe in God and believe all that he has said and revealed to us, and that Holy Church proposes for our belief, because he is truth itself."[374] Faith is that quality of the human heart that believes without fully understanding because of the love that we have for the One who informs us. Yes, faith seeks understanding, but we will never fully understand God: He is infinite, and we are not.

---

372 CCC ¶1808.
373 CCC ¶1809.
374 CCC ¶1814.

When God called Abram out of the land of Ur, Abram had no idea what lay before him, but he put his faith in God, and God credited it to him as righteousness, as holiness.[375] Abram did not know what God was calling him to, but in faith, Abraham followed, and he is called our father in faith. With Abraham, we can see faith as the beginning of our pilgrimage to God.

Hope: "Hope is the theological virtue by which we desire the kingdom of heaven and eternal life as our happiness, placing our trust in God's promises and relying not on our own strength, but on the help of the grace of the Holy Spirit." [376] The Catechism goes on to say that hope corresponds "to the aspiration to happiness which God has placed in the heart of every man...." [377]

Deep in our hearts, we all seek happiness. Very often, our society crushes it, or deceives us into pursuing things that will not make us ultimately happy, but will only lead us to despair and hopelessness, attributes of Hell. But the hope that God has placed in our hearts will lead us to the ultimate happiness, being with God for all eternity in Heaven.

Charity: "Charity is the theological virtue by which we love God above all things for his own sake, and our neighbor as ourselves for the love of God." [378] Charity is the cement of all the other virtues: "[a]nd over all these put on love, that is, the bond of perfection." [379] It is charity that raises human love to divine love.[380] If we practice virtue out of fear, we are slaves; if we practice virtue for the sake of what we will get for it, we are merce-

375 Gen. 15:6; Rom. 4:1-25; and Gal. 3:6-9.
376 CCC ¶1817.
377 CCC ¶1818.
378 CCC ¶1822.
379 Col. 3:14.
380 CCC ¶1827.

naries; but if we practice virtue out of love, we become children of God.[381] St. Paul tells us[382] that without charity, we are nothing, we gain nothing. Charity is the crown of all virtues; it is what gives significance to everything that we do, and even to who we are. Faith and hope are critical in this life, but in Heaven, when we see God face to face, only love will remain.[383] So love one another.[384]

And as the Catechism tells us, "all works of perfect Christian virtue spring from love and have no other objective than to arrive at love."[385] As I mentioned at the beginning of this section on holiness, perfect charity constitutes holiness.[386] So the commandments and works of mercy help us to grow in virtue; perfect Christian virtue springs from and is directed at love; and love is the foundation, the essence, of holiness.

---

381 CCC ¶1828.
382 1 Cor. 13:1 and ff.
383 1 Cor. 13:13.
384 John 13:34.
385 CCC ¶25.
386 See CCC ¶1709.

PART FOUR

Sacrifice

*"True and perfect love for the crucified Lord so esteems
conformity with him that it regards suffering for God
as a very great gift and reward."* [387]

*"I have been crucified with Christ;
yet I live, no longer I, but Christ lives in me."* [388]

---

387 From John of Avila, *Audi Filia - Listen, O Daughter*, Paulist Press 2006, quoted from Magnificat February
2018, Vol. 19, No. 12
388 Cf. Gal. 2:19-20.

So we started by considering prayer, the way that we develop our relationship with God. Then we considered holiness which can be viewed as our response to getting to know and love God. Now we need to turn to our interaction with the world, and that necessarily involves suffering.

We live in a world full of suffering – poverty, disease, warfare, crime, deadly storms. It seems to be ingrained in our very existence. Although the Saints have intensely loved God and their fellow men, they have not been immune to suffering. In fact while we try to avoid it, the Saints have seemed to embrace it. How do we make sense of this? To help understand the mystery of suffering, I want to start looking at suffering with a story.

Blessed Margaret of Castello[389]

Margaret (†1320) was born into a world very different from what we know. There was no hot or cold running water. There was no indoor plumbing (chamber pots were just emptied into the streets). There was no heating or air conditioning. They had no idea how diseases were spread or the importance of just washing hands. People could die from a cold or a flu or even from a scratch if it got infected. Many women and children died in childbirth. Infant mortality rates were high. People rarely lived to 50.

In some ways, the world was very small. Unless a traveler happened to come through town, you really only knew what was go-

---

ing on in the immediate surrounding neighborhood, town, city, or countryside.

Life was ruled by city-states. If a city grew powerful enough, it would control some of the country around it. And in order to increase its power and influence, one town might attack a nearby town to try to get control of it, but it couldn't be very far away. And since everyone's safety depended on the person who was in charge of the city, that prince was really important.

Margaret was the daughter of one of those princes. Her parents, Parisio and Emilia, wanted a strapping young son who would be able to take over the city when Parisio grew old. Instead they got Margaret. Margaret was a very disabled girl; she was a midget; she had a hunched back; her right leg was much shorter than her left; and she was blind.

Parisio and Emilia were incredibly selfish and vain. Margaret was an embarrassment to them, so they hid her from everyone. No one in the castle was allowed to talk about her. They only had her baptized because the local priest insisted. They sent her to be baptized with the maid who picked her name because her parents couldn't be bothered.

When she was six years old, Margaret was almost discovered by some visitors to the castle. Her parents were horrified, so they decided to lock her away in a small cell attached to a church in the forest. She was kept there like an animal and fed through a small slot in the wall. Her only comfort during this time was a priest who would come to visit. He told her how much God loved her, and how Jesus had died for her. Margaret identified closely with Christ in His suffering, but not in a self-pitying sort of a way. She developed a deep love of Christ and His Passion. When she was twelve, a neighboring prince started to invade Parisio's area, so out of fear that Margaret might be discovered, Parisio moved her to a castle in another city that was farther away, and he locked her in the dungeon.

When Margaret was about twenty, her mother heard about a Franciscan layman who had recently died. People were reporting that miracles were occurring at his grave. Emilia told Parisio about it. Although neither of them were religious, they decided to give this a shot. Early one morning, under strict secrecy, they left their home taking Margaret with them and ventured over the mountains to Castello, the town where the Franciscan was buried. They deposited Margaret close to his grave, told her to pray for a miracle, and then left. When they came back several hours later and saw that no miracle had occurred, they left again –without Margaret. Margaret, the blind, crippled, midget became a street urchin.

She was befriended by some other beggars and was taken in by some poor families. Despite everything that had happened to her, everyone saw that she had the sweetest disposition and was a very devout soul. She developed a reputation as a holy person and became a sort of personality in Castello. A community of nuns took note of this and invited her to join them. However, while Margaret wanted to live a religious life, there was little prayer, virtually no silence, and no real poverty in the convent. Margaret tried to live her religious vows, which angered the other nuns who threw her out and slandered her publicly. Margaret, back on the streets, said nothing.

Believing the nuns, the town originally looked at Margaret as a fraud. But as time went on, they saw Margaret was the one who was living her faith under very difficult circumstances. Not only was she not complaining, but she was thanking God for allowing her to suffer like Christ had done.

Soon a group of Dominican laywomen took note of her and asked her to join them. This was a group of women who took their faith and their promises very seriously. Finally after so many years and so many trials, Margaret found her home. She spent her time praying, taking care of the sick, and visiting prisons. There were numerous cures and conversions attributed to her. She continued to pray for long hours, fast regularly, and thank God for the many trials that she suffered.

Margaret died when she was only 33. Miracles followed within hours of her death. She was immediately acclaimed a saint by the citizens of Castello, although Rome took a lot longer just to proclaim her "Blessed." Although she died in 1320, her incorrupt body is still on display at the School for the Blind in Citta di Castello, Italy.

People like Margaret pose a real challenge to our modern society. She was crippled, blind, deformed, and ugly. Most people in our society would have viewed her as unfortunate at best, and at worst as cursed. It is reported that when Margaret was still a child, the people in her hometown said she should never have been born, and I can imagine people saying that sort of thing today. Yet it seems that Margaret rejoiced in her sufferings and even practiced severe penances on top of what she naturally had to handle. To our minds, that doesn't make any sense. How do we sort it all out?

The Problem of Evil

The existence of evil in the world is a huge stumbling block for many people in our society. Recently a celebrity on social media offered to pray for a fellow celebrity who had suffered a severe heart attack. He was roundly condemned and mocked by several people for his audacity to suggest prayer. One comment in particular asked if this "god" of his had inflicted the heart attack on the friend as some sort of a cruel joke. The post went on to blame all of the evils in the world on this sadistic "god." As I said, the existence of evil in the world is a problem for people's belief in God. So I think it would be useful to give some thought to it.

Here is the problem: if God is all-powerful, and if He is all-loving, then there should not be any evil or pain or suffering in the world. But we all know that bad things happen to good, innocent people. So this means that either God is not good; or that He is not all powerful; or that God does not exist at all. Right?

You might want to read that again. It is the root of the problem of evil. The existence of evil and pain and suffering in the world is one of the big reasons that people do not believe in God. We need to try to understand why there is evil in the world.[390]

The Origin of Suffering

In the biblical story of creation, we hear how God created the light, and He saw that it was good; He created the sky; He created the dry lands and the seas, and He saw that it was good; He

---

390 If you're interested in reading more on this subject, please see Peter Kreeft, *Making Sense out of Suffering*, Servant Books, 1986.

created the stars, the moon, and the sun, and He saw that it was good; He created fish, birds, and all of the animals, and He saw that it was good; and then he created man, both male and female, and He saw that it was good. God created everything. And when God was finished with all creation, the Bible says, "God looked at everything He had made, and found it was *very good*." [391]

So if everything God created is good, where does evil come from? As St. John tells us, "God is love." [392] The problem with love is that it cannot be forced. Forced love is counterfeit. More than anything, God wants us to love Him with a pure, unadulterated love.

Since God is love, and all he wants is to be loved in return, He had to give all of His intelligent creatures (angels and humans) free will. In order to love Him, we had to be free to reject Him and to love ourselves more than Him. That is always the risk of loving – not being loved in return. As we all know, that has not played out so well.

When God put Adam and Eve in the Garden of Eden, He said they could eat the fruit of any of the trees that were in the garden except for the fruit from the tree of the knowledge of good and evil. [393] Since God wants us to love Him, He gave Adam and Eve the ability not to love Him, to disobey Him. So He put that tree in the center of the Garden.

Satan tempted Adam and Eve. [394] The temptation was not so much an invitation to openly rebel against God; Satan is far too crafty for that. Instead, he said that if they ate from that tree, "...

---

391 Gen 1:31. (Emphasis added.)
392 1 John 4:8.
393 Gen. 2:16-17.
394 Gen. 3.6.

your eyes will be opened and *you will be like gods*, who know good from evil."[395]

If we think about it, it is the height of arrogance to want to be like God. God is like no other. St. Anselm of Canterbury once wrote in his book the *Proslogion* that God is the being of whom nothing greater can be conceived. No one can be "like Him."

It is hard to understand the sin of Adam and Eve. They had everything they could possibly want. However, they must have realized that they were totally dependent on God for everything, which is true for all of us. Satan's temptation was the illusion (the lie) that Adam and Eve could become free from that dependence. Adam and Eve seemed to have wanted something more than they had. And if we want something more, in a sense, we are dissatisfied (maybe in a very subtle way) with what we have. So Adam and Eve must in some way have been dissatisfied with the status quo and wanted to be independent, or that temptation would not have been effective. Adam and Eve were dissatisfied with their condition; they rejected the reality that they were totally dependent on God for everything (the only true reality); they chose to strive for independence – to be "like God."

But there is a catch, a consequence. God is the source of all truth, beauty, and love. God is also real. Indeed, God is the only reality. If we push away from God, we push away from all of that. We push into chaos. And that is what we have around us now.

After Adam and Eve disobeyed God, He visited them and confronted them. He told them the consequence of their sin: Eve would bear children in pain and suffering; work became difficult; and death entered the world.[396]

---

395 Gen. 3:4. (Emphasis added.)
396 Gen. 3:16-19.

So according to Genesis, the evil in the world is the consequence of the choice Adam and Eve made against God – that is sin. Sin is, in effect, our effort to push away from God. We are saying, "No" to God, and "Yes" to ourselves. That attitude is at the heart of every sin we commit: I want it my way, not God's. We are trying to make ourselves "like god." Since God gave us our free will, He will respect our choice.

The Consequences of Sin

Some will protest that sin is personal, and the consequence of sin should be personal as well, but that is not what the Bible teaches us. Adam and Eve sinned, and the consequences were pain, suffering, and death. However, their punishment was not just theirs – all of us suffer from and need forgiveness for that Original Sin.

In some mysterious way, Original Sin seems to have disrupted, wrinkled, or even torn the very fabric of our universe. Not just the spiritual world, but even the physical world. As St. Paul says in Romans:

> *"For creation awaits with eager expectation the revelation of the children of God; for creation was made subject to futility, not of its own accord, but because of the one who subjected it, in hope that creation itself would be set free from slavery to corruption and share in the glorious freedom of the children of God."* [397]

Because of the sin of Adam and Eve, all of creation is broken to a certain extent.[398] Of course, God continues to shine through a sunrise, a sunset, the song of a bird. But snakebites can be dead-

---

397 Rom. 8:19-21.
398 CCC ¶397-401.

ly; some plants are poisonous; there are diseases. What God created was good. The Bible says it was "very good." The evil in the world did not come from God: evil, pain, and suffering began with Original Sin.

St. Augustine says that one of the consequences of Original Sin is that all of us have a tendency to sin. He called it "concupiscence." In contemporary society that term suggests sexual desire, but as mentioned above, concupiscence refers to all of our disordered desires. So concupiscence is that tendency in us to turn from God and choose ourselves ... and sin.

In addition, the nature of sin has not changed over time. When we sin, we push ourselves away from God, away from the only true reality, into chaos and spiritual isolation. The more that people sin, the more we are all isolated in the chaos that is self-love, or the root of Hell.

So our personal sins do not only affect us; they affect all of creation. It's like the rock thrown into a pond; the ripples caused by the rock spread to every shore. That's how it works with our sins. When we sin, we contribute to the disorder of the world. By that I mean that we push away from what God designed the world, the entire universe, to be. Since He is God (and we are not), if we move the universe away from its Creator, we move it more and more into chaos. We may think of our little sins as insignificant, but every sin (no matter how small) does in fact matter.

Fortunately, Jesus gave us the sacrament of confession for God to wipe away our sins. The Psalms tell us that, "As far as the east is from the west, so far has he removed our sins from us."[399] St. Augustine tells us that God forgives our venial sins just

---

399 Psalms 103:12.

by our sincerely praying the Our Father. Attending Mass is a tremendous source of grace and forgiveness as well. God wants to forgive our sins. We just have to ask. We are all weak, and even if we convinced everyone to repent, being imperfect as we are, we will continue to sin.

But not everyone will ask. Our world will continue to be burdened by evil, by suffering. And the innocent will often bear the burden.

God created everything good. He did not create pain and suffering and evil. Pain and suffering came from Original Sin and continue to come from our continuing, ongoing sin. When we sin, we push God away and push ourselves into chaos. And that is the root, the origin, of pain, suffering, and the evil in the world.

But we as Christians trust in God; by doing so, we have hope, even in the midst of terrible suffering. In fact, Christ assured us that anyone who suffered for the sake of righteousness or because of Him is truly blessed.[400] To an unbeliever, that is utter nonsense. To a believer, it is a sustaining belief in the promise of sacrifice.

The Snakes in Our Lives

We know that Christ suffered His Passion and died a terrible, humiliating death on the Cross to save us from "death," to redeem us. But what does that really mean?

The Prophet Isaiah writes many beautiful things about the Kingdom of God. He writes about how the people will beat their swords into plowshares and their spears into pruning hooks. One nation will not raise a sword against another, and people

---

400 Matt. 5: 10-11.

will not train for war again.[401] The wolf will lie down with the lamb; the leopard with the young goat; the calf and the young lion will graze together with a child leading them. Children will play around poisonous snakes and not be harmed.[402]

Our reality is very different. Isaiah's words don't capture the world that I experience. I don't think it is the world that anyone of us experiences. Isaiah is talking about Heaven, and though I hope that we are all on our way to Heaven, we aren't there yet.

So where exactly are we?

In the book of Numbers, there is a strange story about what God did to the Israelites when they were in the desert. They had been eating manna and quail for quite some time. I would imagine that eating the same thing day after day would get old. It probably lost its taste and became unappetizing. I'm not sure what spices were available in the desert. There is nothing in the Bible about a manna and quail cookbook. So the Israelites complained against God. In response, the Lord sent poisonous snakes among them, seraph serpents.

I tried to find out what these snakes were, but the term doesn't seem to refer to any known species of snakes. So what are they? They were snakes, of course, but the word "seraph" is used as an adjective describing the snakes. Seraph is an uncommon word in the Bible, but when it is used it refers to angels who are close to God. God is described as a blazing fire, so we could assume that the Seraphim are similarly ablaze. So perhaps the seraph serpent's bite caused a burning pain?

Many Israelites were bitten and died. The people soon realized their mistake and repented. They asked Moses to pray to God for

---

401 Isaiah 2:4.
402 Isaiah 11:6-9.

them. "Pray to the LORD to take away the serpents from us." [403] And so, Moses prayed for the Israelites.

God answered their prayer, but certainly not in the way they had hoped. God did not take the snakes away like the Israelites had asked. He did not make the snakes non-poisonous or painless. He did not stop the snakes from biting the Israelites. He could have done any of those things. Instead, God told Moses to sculpt a bronze serpent and put it on a pole. [404] He just gave them a cure. Whenever anyone was bitten by a snake, if they would just look at the bronze serpent, they would be healed.

We are told that Jesus triumphed over death. But people still suffer and die. People still get sick as we saw most recently with the COVID-19 pandemic. Bad things still happen to good people and innocent children: sickness and disease; war; abuse.

We pray and pray and pray that God will deliver us from all of these bad things, heal the diseases, and stop the atrocities, but sometimes, it seems that God doesn't hear our prayers. This can cause people to lose hope and despair. Some people become angry with God.

But God *has* answered our prayers: He sent us Jesus. But He did not take away the suffering. We still live in a broken world. But He tells us that if we just keep our eyes focused on the Cross and Resurrection, our suffering will eventually be overcome. [405]

Many people mock Catholics for our supposed preoccupation with suffering. It's almost as if they see us as masochists who enjoy suffering for its own sake. The truth is that Catholics simply acknowledge that suffering is all around us and must

---

403 Numbers 21:7.
404 Many of the Church Fathers saw this as a symbol of Christ's crucifixion.
405 Numbers 21:8-9.

be dealt with according to the will of God. As Dorothy Day once said, "It is not a cult of suffering. It is an acceptance of the human condition." [406]

In this regard, I think it is important to note that God is not insensitive to our suffering. When Christ was at the tomb of Lazarus, he wept.[407] Our suffering is the result of our own sin, and it breaks God's heart. He wept. But in some mysterious way, He uses the consequence of sin to defeat sin; He uses the suffering caused by Satan to defeat Satan.

The Cross

Whenever we enter a Catholic church, we should see a crucifix. I know that some of the more modern churches may have some abstract representation, but it represents the crucified Christ. Protestant churches, on the other hand, have empty crosses, not a crucifix. Paul in writing to the Galatians who were straying into observing Jewish practices mentions that they had a crucifix where they gathered: "O stupid Galatians! Who has bewitched you, before whose eyes Jesus Christ was *publicly portrayed as crucified*?" [408] But the reason the crucifix is in every Catholic church throughout the world is to visually remind us what we are doing in Mass and what is happening.

The cross of Christ is not an option for Christians in general, but particularly not for Catholics. When Jesus and the Apostles went to Caesarea Philippi, He asked them who people said that He was. They had various answers.

---

406 Servant of God Dorothy Day, *Dorothy Day Selected Writings*, Robert Ellsberg, Ed., Orbis Books, Maryknoll, N.Y.

407 John 11:35.

408 Galatians 3:1. [Emphasis added.]

Then He asked them who they said He was. It was Peter who said, "You are the Christ, the Son of God." In response, Christ said, "Blessed are you Peter for no man has revealed that to you but my Father in Heaven."

Jesus, however, immediately told his Apostles that He would have to suffer the Passion. Peter took Jesus aside and told him that would never happen. Jesus' response was emphatic: "Get behind me Satan!" [409] There was Jesus calling Peter (who just proclaimed Him as the Christ) Satan. There is no mistake: the cross was central to the mission of Christ. His crucifixion, His total submission to the will of His Father, was His victory, His glorification.

But Jesus did not plan to do this alone. He repeatedly told His disciples, "Come, after me." [410] More to the point, he said, "Whoever wishes to come after me must deny himself, take up his cross, and follow me." [411] And this was not a "one-and-done" kind of thing. He said that we have to do this daily: "If anyone wishes to come after me, he must deny himself and take up his cross *daily* and follow me." [412] And this was the understanding of the Apostles. [413]

We should expect suffering if we are walking with God. The Cross is not an option. It is a daily call from Jesus, a requirement if we are to be his followers.

The Point of Suffering

So if suffering is inevitable while we are here on earth, and if Christ calls us to the Cross daily, what is the point of it?

---

409 Matt. 16:23.
410 Matt. 4:19; Mark 1:17; 10:21; Luke 5:27; John 1:43 and 21:19.
411 Matt. 16:24.
412 Luke 9:23. [Emphasis added.]
413 1 Peter 2:21.

As bad as suffering can be, there are positive things that can come out of it. For instance, when a person is confronted with suffering, it usually causes him or her to stop and think about their lives and the lives of those around them. People will reflect on what they are doing with their lives and with whom they are spending their time. Sometimes they begin to realize that what they're doing is pointless. They may decide to pursue another more meaningful path. This can be a moment of conversion. As the Venerable Archbishop Fulton Sheen once said, "Sometimes the only way the good Lord can get into some hearts is to break them."

We have a track record of suffering-induced conversions in the Church. When St. Ignatius Loyola was young, he dreamed of being a gallant soldier, a knight in shining armor. It was the thing back then. But during a battle with French forces, he was hit in the leg with a cannonball which broke his leg in two places. The French were so impressed with his military valor that they put him in a cart and took him to his home to recover – over a mountain range. When he arrived, his leg had set crooked, so he had them re-break it. When it set a second time, it was again crooked. Apparently he was upset that his leg would look bad in the stockings they wore, so he had the doctors reset it by breaking it again, certainly without anesthetics. That seems incredibly vain to me.

While he was convalescing, he asked for books about the adventures of chivalrous knights, but he was told that the household only had *The Imitation of Christ* by Thomas a Kempis and books on the lives of the saints, so he was stuck reading those to pass the time. But as time went on, something happened. He grew to realize that the real heroes are the Saints. When his leg was healed, he left the castle a changed man, a converted man. He went on to be a Christian hero, a Saint.

But there is another, personal aspect of suffering that even affects more mature Catholics. Some people (good friends and loved ones) have left the Catholic Church because they were not "getting anything out of it." They perhaps went to a non-denominational service that made them feel good. It was entertaining. It gave them an emotional high. They made friends, and they socialized together. All of that may be nice, but it misses the point in at least two ways, one personal and one communal.

First, emotions can be misleading. There are a lot of people who follow their emotions and end up in the ditch. I don't think we should live our lives just following our emotions. They can lead us astray and ultimately to sadness and disenchantment. True love is not based on an emotional high. True love is an act of the will. It is a bare, naked, selfless affection for another person. God is pure love. He is, in a sense, constrained by love. All He really wants is for you and me to love Him in return.

When we are confronted with difficult times in our spiritual journey, we can have a couple of reactions. One reaction is just to want to give up like the Israelites as they journeyed through the desert. Each time that they faced difficulties — when they were caught between the Red Sea and the advancing Egyptian army;[414] or when they were hungry;[415] or when they were thirsty[416] — they were ready to go back to Egypt. Each time they asked Moses, wouldn't they have been better off in Egypt as slaves rather than

---

414 Exodus 14:11
415 Exodus 16:3
416 Exodus 17:3

be where they were under those particular circumstances.[417]

The Church Fathers saw Egypt as a symbol of the world in contrast to Heaven, or at least to the spiritual life. The slavery of Egypt was seen as an image of our slavery to sin. They saw the sufferings of the Israelites in the desert as comparable to the suffering we must endure to be purged from our own sinfulness, our own self-love.

So many times in our own spiritual journeys when confronted with challenges, such as our sufferings, we are tempted to give up – to just live a worldly life, to just conform. But one of the lessons we learn from the journey of the Israelites is that unless we pass through the desert with all of its challenges, we cannot enter the Promised Land.

When we begin to grow in our faith-life, when our eyes are opened, when we are converted, God many times will fill our lives with spiritual consolations, sort of spiritual highs, like during the honeymoon stage of a marriage. But as we grow in our faith and our love, God often tends to remove those supports to help us to love Him even more purely. It's like a child learning to walk. At first, mom or dad holds his or her hands and supports the child. As the child gets more and more steady on his or her feet, then mom or dad slowly takes a hand away or lessens the support. Finally mom and dad let go, and the child walks on his or her own, a little shaky at first (with mom and dad ready to catch them), but growing stronger with every step. That's how God helps us early in our faith journey. But that doesn't go on forever.

In commenting on the first letter of St. John, St. Augustine

---

417 Exodus 14:12, 16:3, and 17:3.

uses what I think is a good analogy to how God helps us to grow in our faith. If you receive wine or grain, Augustine wrote, you need something to put it in. Before putting new stuff in the old container, you first need to clean it out, to empty it of all of the old debris that might be in it. If your container is not big enough, then you need to stretch it.[418]

God is, of course, infinite. To make room for Him in our hearts, we need to clean out all of the old debris. Some of it may be old, moldy, and rotten, but some of it might just be of lesser quality. God wants to put something much better in its place. To clean out the debris, there might be some painful scraping and loss. God is infinite, and to make room, there could also be some painful stretching.

Jesus' encounter with the Canaanite woman is perhaps a good example of how God will draw us out and stretch us spiritually. The woman comes to Jesus desperately begging for Him to heal her daughter. He didn't say a word to her. His disciples told Him to send her away. He responds by saying that he was only sent to the Jews. But she approaches Him, does Him homage, and begs Him to help her. He says, "It is not right to take the food of the children and throw it to the dogs." [419] He comes across as pretty severe with her. Undaunted, she continues to persist and says, "Please, Lord, for even the dogs eat the scraps that fall from the table of their masters." [420]

By talking to her in this way, Christ drew out of this pagan woman a great faith in Him and perseverance in prayer which was in stark contrast to the faith of the Jewish people. Because of

418 St. Augustine, Tractates on John, Tract. 4: PL 35, 2008-2009.
419 Matthew 15:26.
420 Matthew 15:27.

her faith which she had to act on, He answers her prayer.[421]

Sometimes that is how it is with us. God forces us to make that act of faith. By making that act of faith, we grow closer to Him. But for that act of faith, we would not have grown. Maybe it's a little like getting thrown into the lake and being told, "sink or swim." We learn to swim. The same is true in prayer. Just because Jesus doesn't answer our prayers immediately doesn't mean we should give up. It just means that we need to pray more. God may be using that as a way to draw us closer to Him.

Dante Alighieri (†1321) was an Italian poet. He wrote an epic poem that has come to be known as the *Divine Comedy*. The poem is divided into three sections, one for Hell, one for Purgatory, and one for Heaven. In the poem, Dante travels through hell and Purgatory led by the Roman poet Virgil. Virgil, being a pagan, cannot go beyond Purgatory, so he is led through Heaven by Beatrice, the ideal woman who is based on an actual woman Dante knew.

When Dante enters through the gates of Hell in *The Inferno*, but before he enters into Hell proper, he encounters a large group of souls wailing in various languages. Virgil, his guide, explains that these are the people who were neither rebellious nor faithful to God. He says that the heavens drive them out, but Hell refuses to receive them as well.[422] These are the souls of the people who refused to make a commitment, who said no to the act of faith.[423]

We can see this dynamic of God drawing us out to greater and

---

421 Matt. 15:21-28.
422 *Inferno*, Canto III, vv. 20-50.
423 See Rev. 3:16.

deeper love in the lives of the Saints. People were somewhat surprised (some even scandalized) by a book that came out soon after the death of Mother Teresa: *Mother Teresa: Come Be My Light.*[424] This is a collection of her private writings. In them, she wrote about how dry and empty her prayer had been ... for decades. St. John of the Cross, the passionate Spanish mystic, a doctor of the Church, also wrote about long dry spells in his prayer life. And Theresa of Lisieux once told her sister, Celine, that she had spent seven years without prayerful consolation. Theresa even questioned whether God was hearing her prayers at one point, but she persevered out of a pure love for God and for Him alone. Celine referred to Theresa's faith as "naked faith."

During these times, God did not leave the Saints. He withdrew spiritual consolations from them and drew them out to love Him without those consolations. God wants us to love Him not for what He gives us, but for Him alone. He wants to purge us of all of our attachments to created things that we cling to. He wants us to love Him without crutches.

St. Francis de Sales said that God wants us to love Him with a mature, powerful love that really gets nothing in return. He said, "He wants you to serve him without joy, without feeling, with repugnance and revulsion of spirit. Such service gives you no satisfaction, but it pleases him; it is not according to your liking, but according to his." [425]

I believe that is how Jesus loved God the Father. When He was hanging on the cross, He felt abandoned. He died a terribly painful, humiliating death. Everyone around Him was mocking him,

---

424 Image Books, 2009.
425 *St. Francis de Sales, Selected Letters,* Elisabeth Stopp, Tr. © 1960, Elisabeth Stopp, Harper Brothers Publishers, New York, NY, all rights reserved, quoted in Magnificat, January 2017, Vol. 18, No. 11, page 339.

except for St. Dismas (the good thief) and the few at the foot of the Cross. Almost every one of His Apostles, and all of his disciples, abandoned Him. When He was arrested, they scattered like chickens. And worse than anything else, He could no longer feel the Father's presence. "My God! My God! Why have you forsaken me?" [426] And yet, if He couldn't *feel* the Father's presence, he still *knew* that the Father was there - which is why He cried out to Him. With that knowledge, He persevered out of love for His Father. He never stopped loving Him. And that is what we are called to do.

In *The Practice of the Love of Jesus Christ*, St. Alphonsus Liguori talks about the benefits of patiently enduring the sufferings that God allows: "God rejoices in our suffering in hopes that by enduring it with patience and resignation we may give him proof of our love." [427]

Similarly, St. Alphonsus quotes one of his contemporaries, Fr. Antonio Torres: "Carrying the cross without consolation makes souls fly to heaven." [428] In a sense, loving God through suffering perfects and completes our love of Him. It melts away the dross of self-love that infects us all.

The personal nature of suffering can bring us to God (conversion). It can also help us to grow in and strengthen our love of God (spiritual growth).

As the author of the Letter to the Hebrews says, suffering is to be expected. God disciplines those whom He loves. [429] So when we are confronted with difficulties in our spiritual journey, we

---

426 Matt. 27:46.
427 *The Practice*, p. 84.
428 *The Practice*, Chapter VIII, Section 21, p. 84, quoting from Ludovico Sabbatini d"Anfora, *Vita del Padre D. Antonio Torres*, Preposito Gen. della Cong. d' Pii Operai (Naples, 1732) book 4, ch. 1, pp. 290-291.
429 Heb. 12: 5-7.

can either give up (like the Israelites wanted to do in the desert) or persevere and grow like the Saints.

But as I mentioned, there is another aspect of suffering that is *communal* in nature.

There is a very intriguing passage in Paul's letter to the Colossians. Right after his greeting, he says, "Now I rejoice in my sufferings for your sake, and in my flesh *I am filling up what is lacking* in the afflictions of Christ on behalf of his body, which is the church...." [430]

This is a confusing verse for many evangelicals. Growing up in Texas, I was surrounded by evangelical Christians. One of their oft-repeated phrases was "once saved, always saved." For them, Jesus' sacrifice on the Cross was complete and totally sufficient for our salvation. The idea that we need to fill "up what is lacking" in His sacrifice would not have made sense. It suggests that there is something lacking in the sacrifice of Christ on the Cross. It suggests that Christ did not offer the perfect, complete, and total sacrifice. But we all know that He did. We know that His was the perfect sacrifice that redeemed all of mankind. So what does this passage mean?

One time I asked a priest friend of mine what that passage meant, and he explained that what Paul meant was that each of us is called to the Cross, to join with Jesus in the sacrifice on Calvary: what is lacking in His suffering is you and me joining our suffering to His.

Jesus said: "Come. Follow Me." We are being invited by Christ to join Him in His sacrifice to redeem the world. In a way, we are like Simon the Cyrenean who, coming in from the country,

---

430 Col. 1:24. [Emphasis added.]

stumbled onto Jesus carrying His cross, and was forced to help.[431] We are being asked to help to carry the Cross of Christ. What an incredible honor and privilege He is giving to us!

The Morning Offering

How exactly do we help Christ to carry the Cross? How do we unite our sufferings to the sacrifice of Christ? How do we take advantage of the little (and great) sufferings that come our way? How do we turn our worthless suffering into valuable sacrifices?

In the mid-1800s, there was Jesuit seminary in the town of Vals, France. Vals is a tiny village in southwestern France near the border of Spain. It has a current population of about 85 souls, and it wasn't much bigger in the 1800's.

The seminarians were studying for missionary work in India and America. They knew all about the stories of Sts. Isaac Jogues (†1646) and Jean de Brebeuf (†1649) who traveled to what is now New York to minister to the native Americans and were tortured and brutally killed for their efforts; and of St. Francis Xavier who traveled to the Far East converting tens of thousands in Japan and India. I'm sure they were on fire to spread the Gospel. But there they were studying in little Vals, France (probably not much happening there). It is probably a gross understatement to say that they were anxious.

Their spiritual advisor at the seminary was a certain Fr. Francis X. Gautrelet, S.J. (†1886). He recognized the seminarians' anxiety. In reflecting on Colossians 1:23-24, he realized that the seminarians could put all of that worry, that spiritual energy in a way, to good use. He told the students to offer it up;

---

431 Matt. 27:32; Mark 15:21-22; and Luke 23:26.

to offer everything up: their prayers, their works, their joys, their sufferings.

This was not a new idea in the Church. But the prayer that Fr. Gautrelet composed for the seminarians was. He told them that they should begin each day by offering the day to the Lord. We know the prayer as "The Morning Offering":

> *Oh my Jesus,*
> *Through the Immaculate Heart of Mary,*
> *I offer you my prayers, works, joys, and sufferings of this day*
> *In union with the Holy Sacrifice of the mass throughout the world.*
> *I offer them for all of the intentions of Your Sacred Heart:*
> *For the salvation of souls, in reparation for sin, and for the reunion*
>   *of all Christians.*
> *I offer them for the intentions of our bishops and of all members of*
>   *the Apostleship of Prayer*
> *And in particular for the intentions of the Holy Father.*
> *And I offer them for the intentions of my family and friends.*[432]

We might believe that we are not in a position to do anything great. When we think of Christian suffering, what probably comes to mind is the martyrdom of the Saints: St. Stephen being stoned to death; St. Peter being crucified upside down; St. Bartholomew being flayed; St. Joan of Arc being burned at the stake; St. Thomas More being beheaded.

Others may think of Christian suffering as the severe penances that some monks and nuns practiced in the Middle Ages – long fasts, sleepless nights in prayer, or self-flagellation (this is ex-

---

432 There are several versions of this prayer that can be found on the Internet such as one from EWTN and the USCCB websites. This version is based on the one used by the Jesuits at the Whitehouse Retreat Center in St. Louis, though I added the last sentence.

treme asceticism). Some of these things are hard for us to understand in our current environment, but it was a very different time and place.

Or still others may have in mind the heroic sufferings of some of our Saints, like Bernadette Soubirous. Bernadette is famous as the poor girl to whom Our Lady of Lourdes appeared. When told by Our Lady to dig, she

The Apostleship of Prayer is the organization started in 1844 by the Jesuit seminarians of Vals, France, to promote this devotion. It has been recognized by the Pope and has spread worldwide. The Pope each month announces his prayer intention for the Apostleship. It has been nicknamed the Papal prayer group. In 1944, Pope Pius XII said that the Apostleship is one of the most efficacious means for the salvation of souls.

dug in the dirt, and the miraculous, healing waters of Lourdes began to flow.

Soon afterwards, Bernadette disappeared into a convent. She did not revel in the notoriety of the waters. Bernadette's health had never been very good. From childhood she had a weak and sickly constitution and suffered from asthma. And while in the convent, she developed a painful tubercular tumor in the bone of her right knee.

Sometime later visitors came to the convent. They asked her if she knew about the cures at Lourdes and why she didn't take advantage of them. Her response was simple: "You see, my business is to be ill." As Our Lady had told Bernadette, "I do not promise to make you happy in this life, but in the next." There are many Saints[433] who willingly took on suffering. These Saints

---

433 For instance, St. Fina, St. Francis of Assisi, Padre Pio, Venerable Anne Catherine Emmerich, or St. Gemma Galgani.

are sometimes referred to as "victim souls" who offer up all of their sufferings for the salvation of the world.

There are those who suffer the big things: the loss or incurable sickness of a loved one, particularly a child; the premature death of a spouse; or one's own serious illness or debilitating condition. We live in a world full of suffering– illness, pain, and death. But there are also the small things that we suffer. We may fail a test we studied hard for. We might not get the promotion and raise that we really felt that we needed in order to provide for our family ... or worse, we could lose a job. We may be involved in a car wreck. We may get sick. Or we may just stub our toe.

Some of these are minor inconveniences, but they are a small kind of suffering. Yes, some of us bear great suffering; but we all suffer little things on a daily basis.

God doesn't necessarily call us to do great things. In the Gospel of Matthew, Jesus reminds us that not everyone who does great things will enter the kingdom of Heaven.[434] Casting out demons, prophesying, or working mighty deeds will not guarantee admission to the Kingdom.[435] Rather, as He Himself was submissive to the will of His father,[436] He calls us to be submissive to His will so that He can do great things through us right where we are. As Mother Teresa of Calcutta often said, "God does not choose the qualified, but He qualifies the ones He chooses." [437] The important thing in this battle is that we never waste our suffering.

---

434 Matt. 7:22-23.

435 Matt. 7:21-23.

436 Matt. 26:39; Mark 14:36; Luke 22:42; John 6:38; and Psalm 40:7-9.

437 Quoted in *Fatima for Today: The Urgent Marian Message of Hope*, Fr. Andrew Apostoli, C.F.I., Ignatius Press 2010, Loc. 385.

The Mass and Our Sufferings

I once heard a story about Venerable Archbishop Fulton Sheen. While driving by a hospital, he looked up and said, "All that wasted suffering." Yes, suffering is a waste if we do nothing with it, but if we turn it into a sacrifice, it becomes invaluable. This is how we can transform the punishment merited by Original Sin (suffering) and turn it into our means of victory over Satan (sacrifice).

As Catholics, we have an effective way to use our sufferings: the Mass. If we fully participate in the Mass, it is not only Christ who is being sacrificed on the altar, but if we offer to Him all of our prayers, works, joys, and sufferings, we are joining Him in that sacrifice; we are joining Him on the Cross; we are uniting ourselves to His sufferings. Our sufferings are transformed, and we are more and more conformed to the Body of Christ. We become other Christs, *alteri Christi*.

As I discussed earlier when talking about the Mass as prayer, God created time. God is not subject to time. God is outside of time. So although Jesus became man and lived among us, all of His actions had an eternal dimension as well. In the truest sense, His actions were timeless.

Since God is outside of time and the Mass is eternal, then at every Mass, we participate in that eternal, Heavenly Mass. But we are also present at the Crucifixion of Jesus. All of this was in time, but because it was God incarnate suffering, it was also timeless. So the Crucifixion is also an eternal or timeless event. And finally, at Mass, we are present at the Last Supper. At Mass, we step out of time and move into the eternal, the timeless.

When we were baptized, we were joined to the Body of Christ. And when we worthily receive Communion at Mass, we are even more assimilated into the Body of Christ. This is not just some sort of theoretical or spiritual sort of thing. We receive in Communion the actual Body and Blood, Soul and Divinity of Our Lord and Savior, Jesus Christ, and if we cooperate with Him, ever so gradually, over time, we become a part of the actual Body of Christ.

Jesus wants us to unite our sufferings to His and participate in the redemption of the world.[438] It is almost unimaginable, but it is through the Mass that we are given the unbelievable gift of being permitted to join Christ in His redemption of the world. If we offer our sufferings, in union with the Sufferings of Jesus through the Mass, we are no longer just spectators at the Mass; we actually become participants in the sacrifice of the Mass. The Mass is about you and me uniting our sufferings to the Sacrifice of Jesus on Calvary, and participating in the redemption of the world.

But as I've said, God will not force us to do this. He only invites us to do this. We have to actually offer our sufferings to Him at Mass. That prayer can be in the form of the Morning Offering; or it can be a simple request that Jesus use our sufferings for whatever our intention might be, or for the salvation of the world. Our prayer can be as simple as you want, but remember: although we can and should always ask God to free us from our trials, we should be willing to accept His will in everything. So our prayer is not necessarily, "Lord, take my sufferings from

---

438 Matt. 4:19; Mark 1:17; 10:21; Luke 5:27; John 1:43; and 21:19; Matt. 16:24; and Luke 9:23.

me"; but rather, "Lord, use my sufferings for a greater good."
And He certainly will.

Just don't waste your sufferings, great or small. We need them
for the salvation of the world.

The Little Things

I want to return for a moment to Brother Lawrence. He was the
Discalced Carmelite brother in Paris who found prayer in the
hustle and bustle of the priory kitchen. I talked about him in
the section on prayer in regard to how he took what he thought
was all wrong about his life of "prayer" and turned his life into
a prayer.

God puts us right where He wants us to be. He has something
He wants us to do right here, right now. It is something especially designed for you and for me. Brother Lawrence ended up in
the kitchen when he thought he should be in the church praying. By trusting in God, he found out that he was just where God
wanted him to be. Brother Lawrence is a great example of humbly accepting our place in the world, and glorifying even that little corner for God.

We may think that our lives don't matter much because virtually no one outside of our immediate circle of family and
friends even knows us. It's a good thing that Our Blessed Mother didn't think that way. Jerusalem was the center of the Jewish
cultural and religious power. She lived in a tiny village far from
Jerusalem. She was a very humble, simple, but prayerful young
woman, and yet God did not forget her. He chose her to change
the world.

Consider also the first 30 years of our Lord's life. We know
virtually nothing about those "silent" years, and yet I know that

those years were not wasted. When Jesus was baptized, the Holy Spirit came to rest on Him, and a voice from Heaven said, "This is my beloved Son, with whom I am well pleased." [439] I am certain that the Lord accomplished great things in that hidden life. We will never know what those years really meant until we reach the other side of death.

One of the first lay Saints canonized by the Church was St. Isidore the Farmer (†1130). He was a farm laborer all of his life. He would begin each day going to Mass and would faithfully perform his work. But even in this simple, uneventful life, he was fulfilling the will of God, and he was blessed. Many miracles are attributed to him. He might have been forgotten entirely except that through his intercession, King Philip III of Spain was healed of a deadly disease, and on his recovery, he set about to make sure that Isidore was canonized. How many of these simple saints are there around us every day?

One of the greatest recent Saints is Theresa of Lisieux. She lived a simple life. She had hoped to be a missionary, but instead she followed her older sisters into the Discalced Carmelite convent near her home. It was there that she spent the rest of her short life.

As with many religious, her life may have just disappeared into silence but for the fact that her sister, the prioress of the convent, asked her to write her biography as she lay dying of tuberculosis. In it (*The Story of a Soul*[440]), Theresa tells us how to achieve great holiness in the simplest things in our lives. Whether we are scrubbing the floor, doing the dishes, or mending clothes,

---

439 Matt. 3:17; see also Luke 3:22.
440 St. Benedict Press, Tan Books, 2010 (first published 1951 by Burns, Oates and Washbourne).

we should offer it up and do it for the glory of God. That is her "Little Way." God can do great things in us, no matter how small or insignificant we might think we are.

A beautiful prayer reflecting on this truth is Psalm 139. In it, the Psalmist talks about how nothing escapes the notice of God:

"LORD, you have probed me, you know me:
you know when I sit and stand;
you understand my thoughts from afar." [441]

"You formed my inmost being;
you knit me in my mother's womb.
I praise you, because I am wonderfully made;
wonderful are your works!" [442]

God made us for Him and put us right where He wants us to be. We just need to trust in Him and be open to what it is that He wants of us.

Submission to the Will of God

Although fasts and long prayer vigils are good and profitable things, the example of Christ shows us a better way. In the Garden of Gethsemane, Jesus prayed that His Father's will be done, not His. [443] This tells us that although Jesus was fully God, He was also fully human with His own human will. Yet He completely submitted His human will to His own divine will and to that of His Father. In Original Sin, as in all of our personal sins, we want to follow our own will and not God's. The perfect sacrifice of Jesus was His complete and total submission of His human will to the will of His Father.

---

441 Psalm 139:1-2.
442 Psalm 139:13-14.
443 Luke 22:42.

I want to quote St. Alphonsus Liguori again from *The Practice* because he treats suffering in detail. He notes that, "God is pleased by persons who practice mortifications by fasting, hair shirts, and disciplines, because of the courage displayed in such mortifications; but he is much more pleased by those who have the courage to bear patient-

> *Hair shirts were uncomfortable and irritating shirts made out of course cloth which some people would wear as penance or mortification.*

ly and cheerfully the crosses that God sends them." [444] He goes on to say that: "[We] must realize that the involuntary mortifications that God himself sends us are more pleasing to him than the voluntary ones that we take up on our own." [445] He also notes that, "... the most trivial actions, such as working, eating meals, recreating or resting, when done for God's sake, become the gold of holy love." [446] Quoting St. Francis de Sales, St. Alphonsus says, "The mortifications that come to us from God, or from fellow humans with God's permission, are always more precious than those born of our own will. It is a general rule that the less our own choice is involved, the more pleased God is, and the greater profit for ourselves." [447] He goes on to provide a general maxim: "Whatever comes from God, whether it be prosperity or adversity, is good and for our welfare." [448]

Even our illnesses can be looked at as channels of grace. St. Vincent de Paul (†1660) once said, "If we only knew what a pre-

---

444 *The Practice*, p. 51.
445 *The Practice*, p. 209.
446 *The Practice*, p. 67.
447 *The Practice*, p. 51.
448 *The Practice*, p. 216.

cious treasure is contained in sickness, we would greet it with the same joy as we do the greatest blessings." [449]

And St. Teresa of Avila in *The Way of Perfection* wrote that souls would gain "... in a single day, more lasting favors and graces in His Majesty's sight than they could gain in ten years by means of trials which they sought on their own account." [450]

Whatever trials we suffer, whether great or small, we should not waste them. By offering these sufferings to God for our families, for the Church, for our government and its leaders, for the conversion of sinners, for the poor souls in Purgatory, for whatever our intention might be, we convert mere suffering into an invaluable sacrifice, an act of love.

I am reminded of a story my daughter, Kristin, once told me. Just like my wife, she believes in natural child birth without anesthetics. She told me that when she was giving birth to one of her sons, when the pain was great, she offered it up for her soon-to-be-born son. She told me that it didn't make the pain go away, but it changed its character. It became a loving sacrifice that she was offering up for her son, a prayer. We should not waste our suffering.

When confronting suffering in our lives, when things look bleak and perhaps hopeless, we should have the attitude of the Prophet Habakkuk. Writing at the time of the second Babylonian invasion of Israel and the destruction of Jerusalem, he wrote:

> *Though the fig tree blossom not,*
> *Nor fruit be on the vines,*
> *Though the yield of the olive fail,*

---

449 St. Teresa of Avila, *The Way of Perfection*, op. cit.., Kindle p. 151.
450 *The Practice*, p. 151.

And the terraces produce no nourishment,
Though the flocks disappear from the fields,
And there be no herd in the stalls,
Yet I will rejoice in the LORD,
And exult in God my Savior. [451]

It is an amazing thing, but the little sacrifices that we offer up are magnified by the grace of the Cross of Christ. Those great (and even those small) sufferings that God permits us to suffer, if borne patiently, and even cheerfully, can be great moments of grace in our lives. We should not pass up those gifts that God offers to us on a daily basis.

Christ's Passion, Death, and Resurrection are a victory through death. He loved His Father and us through all of His suffering. His victory was the Resurrection after His death.

He calls us to follow Him - to love Him and His Father totally, recklessly, in total and complete faith amid the pain, the suffering, the betrayal, the confusion, the despair and desolation, and yes, even the death that surrounds us each and every day. He invites us to go through this "Passover" with Him to reach the glory of the Resurrection.

It cannot be emphasized enough that it is only through love that we triumph. It is only through a self-abandoning love that we reach the day of the Resurrection, Heaven. There is no room for self-pity, for self-aggrandizement, for self-love in Heaven. For in Heaven, God will be all in all.[452] It is there that all of our hopes and longings and dreams and desires will be su-

---

451 cf. Hab. 3:17-18.
452 1 Cor. 15:28.

per-abundantly fulfilled and satisfied. It is there that our heart longs to go. It is there that we want to be reunited with all of our loved ones.

Just as I opened this section with the story of Margaret of Castello, and I asked how we are supposed to understand the holiness of someone who suffers like that, I close with her example. Margaret became holy by joyfully uniting her suffering to the Cross of Christ, by completing in her own profound suffering the suffering of Christ on the Cross, the perfect sacrifice.

As the result of sin, suffering entered the world. In one way or another, we all experience suffering. It is inescapable. But God, being all-loving and all-powerful, has taken the consequence of sin and transformed it into a way for us to unite ourselves to His Son, Jesus. We in our own large or small ways can grow closer to God, the source of all holiness, by lovingly accepting all of those pains, sicknesses, setbacks, and yes, even deaths that come our way by uniting them to the sufferings of Christ on the Cross through the Mass. That is the profound wisdom we learn from someone like Margaret. That is the profound beauty of sacrifice.

In Summary

As I mentioned in the beginning of this Handbook, the one thing that everyone seems to be able to agree on is that the world is a mess. This seems particularly true for Catholics. I don't know that we have it any worse now than what the early Christians faced with the Roman Empire; than what the early medieval Christians confronted with the Viking and Norse invasions; than what the late medieval and Renaissance Christians faced with the Muslim invasions; or what the faithful French confronted in the French Revolution or the faithful Russians faced with the Communist Revolution. It just seems that with the advances in technology, the attacks are now not so much local as global.

So the world is a mess, and the solutions the world has to offer do not work. We have so much pain and unhappiness and lingering, pervasive emptiness that longs to be filled but seemingly can't. The only real solution is Jesus Christ and his Church, but many people in the world reject Christianity, to say nothing of Catholicism. Our ordinary means of persuasion fail. What is needed is a spiritual conversion - a *metanoia*. We need to turn to spiritual means: prayer, holiness, and sacrifice. It is only through these that we can save the souls of all our loved ones and heal the world.

There are dozens of reasons to do nothing. Fight them! No soul should be left behind.

Don't say you don't have the skills to debate these issues! Do not say you are not smart enough, not educated enough, or not eloquent enough! You may not feel up to the task of an open conflict – engaging in apologetic debates. You may not have the training or the temperament to do that. That's OK. Some of our greatest Saints were very simple people. Think about what God did through St. Joseph who never said a word. We can all participate in this battle by cooperating with God.

Don't say I am just a layperson; that this is not the role of the laity in the Church. Don't say I am not a priest or religious. Venerable Archbishop Fulton Sheen recognized the importance of the laity in this work. In 1972, when addressing the Knights of Columbus at their convention, he asked, "Who is going to save the Church?" "It is the laity," he answered, "by holding our religious, our priests, and even our bishops accountable."

I think that the role of the laity is *more* than just to hold our leaders accountable. The laity has an active role to play. That is what the Church teaches. In *Lumen Gentium*, the Dogmatic Constitution on the Church from the Second Vatican Council, the fathers of the Council said:

> *The lay apostolate, however, is a participation in the salvific mission of the Church itself. ... [T]he laity are called in a special way to make the Church present and operative in those places and circumstanc-*

es where only through them can it become the salt of the earth. *Thus every layman, in virtue of the gifts bestowed upon him, is at the same time a witness and a living instrument of the mission of the Church itself 'according to the measure of Christ's bestowal.'"* [453]

Don't say that the problem is too big or that you are too small. Do not be discouraged by the enormity of the problem. Do not say that you are too young, too old, too sick, or too feeble. When Our Lady of Guadalupe appeared to the peasant Juan Diego, he protested asking her to send someone important and high-born. Our Lady, however, insisted, referring to him as "the smallest of my sons," saying it was necessary that *he* go personally to carry out her wishes. God's ways are not our ways. Offer what you do have to the cause, the little fish and the loaves that you do have, and Jesus will increase it to fill the need. [454]

And don't say that you are too busy. What could be more important than this? Eternal life for you and your loved ones.

We don't have to do everything; in fact, we can't. You and I are minions confronting forces that are more powerful than we can imagine. We are fighting in a very different conflict than what we understand. The fight is not ours alone. We are just called to do our part: pray; live our faith; offer sacrifice; and leave the rest to God.

People, even the irreligious, seem to have a sense of the problem we face and an understanding that it is beyond our own ability to combat the chaos that surrounds us. If we look at contemporary movies and television shows, there are a lot of su-

---

453 *Lumen Gentium* (The Dogmatic Constitution on the Church), Second Vatican Council, ¶33, referring to Matt. 5:13 and Eph. 4:7.
454 Matt. 14:13-21; Luke 9:10-17; and John 6:1-13.

perheroes fighting epic battles against mythic evil forces. We all know that those are make-believe, but I think that they tap into something very primal in us. We have a sense that there is a monumental conflict between good and evil that is going on around us, one that is too big for us as mere humans to overcome, and we don't really understand it. Very often those depictions suggest that the outcome of that conflict will determine the future of mankind, and the superheroes are our saviors.

I once interviewed a priest who said that superheroes really reveal a deep contempt that we feel for ourselves. We know that there is a conflict, but we feel helpless to confront it, so we invent imaginary heroes who can fight those fights for us. There *is* a monumental conflict between good and evil all around us, and there *are* super heroes: the saints. And we are all called to be saints.

Both the Bible and the Saints show us that we are not alone in this fight, but more importantly that it is primarily God's fight, and He only asks us to cooperate.

When the Israelites first arrived at the Promised Land after their many years wandering through the desert, Moses sent spies to investigate what they were facing. The spies came back and reported that although the land flowed with milk and honey, it was inhabited by fierce giants that the Israelites had no hope of defeating.[455] At that time, the Israelites left to wander through the desert because of their lack of faith in God. But later when the Israelites returned to enter the Promised Land, Moses told them not to fear because it was the Lord who would

---

455 Numbers 13:27-28.

destroy these fearsome inhabitants.[456] The fight was not theirs alone, but the Lord's.

During the time of the Judges, Israel was occupied and oppressed by the Midianites, a neighboring kingdom. The Lord sent an angel to call Gideon (I love this guy) to lead the people out of their oppression. Gideon objected saying he was the least in his family which was the poorest in his tribe which was the smallest of the tribes of Israel. But the angel insisted.[457] And when Gideon reluctantly gathered soldiers to fight the Midianites, God told Gideon he had too many soldiers, and he sent most of them away. He said that anyone who was afraid should leave; two-thirds left. But that was still too many. God told Gideon to have the men go down to some water to drink. The men who cupped the water in their hands to drink were sent home, but the ones who lapped up the water like dogs stayed. There were about 300 of those men. With that remnant, God freed Israel.[458]

King Jehoshaphat of Judah (†849 B.C.) was one of the righteous kings of the Old Testament (and not all of them were). He worked hard to destroy the prevalent idol worship and to restore the practices of the Jewish religion. At one point in his reign, several of the surrounding kingdoms decided to join forces to attack Judah. Things looked bleak, so Jehoshaphat turned to God in prayer before the entire assembly of Judah. A prophet stood up and said, "Do not fear or be dismayed at the sight of this vast multitude, for the battle is not yours but God's." [459]

---

456 Deuteronomy 31:2-6.
457 Judges 6:11-21.
458 Judges 7.
459 2 Chronicles 20:15.

The next day when the army of Judah went out to confront the invaders, before the battle began, Jehoshaphat and his troops flanked the invading army and began singing a song of praise to God. And when they sang, the invaders turned on one another and utterly destroyed each other. Judah was saved, but the victory was God's.

St. Theresa Benedicta of the Cross was born Edith Stein, a Jewish girl in an observant Jewish family in what is now Poland. When she was a teenager, she became an atheist. During World War I, she volunteered as a nurse and saw great suffering among the wounded Germans. When she was in college, she became one of the luminaries in a philosophy known as phenomenology. Then, after witnessing the simple faith of working women going into church to pray daily, she began reading some of the works of St. Teresa of Avila. Eventually, she was drawn into the Catholic Church and was baptized in 1922. For some time, she taught in a Catholic school. That was about the time of the rise of Hitler, and the lives of Jews became very difficult. After her conversion she had wanted to enter the Discalced Carmelite Order, and she was finally admitted in 1933.

Theresa fought against the evil that was enveloping Germany, but she recognized that she on her own was fighting a losing battle. She realized that God was calling her to her own Calvary in this fight. She once wrote, "Every time I feel my powerlessness and inability to influence people directly, I become keenly aware of the necessity of my own holocaust." [460] She was arrested and killed in Auschwitz. We are called to a great battle and are guaranteed a great victory. But there is a real price to be paid.

---

460 www.vatican.va/news_services/liturgy/saints/ns_lit_doc_19981011_edith_stein_en.html.

You and I on our own are virtually powerless in this conflict, but we have a secret weapon: Jesus. God has already done the work for us, but all He asks of us is our cooperation. As Jesus told us, apart from Him, we can do nothing.[461] But with Him, we can change the world. As St. Paul tells us, it is in our weakness that the power of Christ is given most fully and manifests itself.[462] If we think we can do things on our own, we only get in the way of God.

I am reminded of the plea of the Psalmist:

"O that my people would listen to me,
that Israel would walk in my ways,
In a moment I would humble their foes;
and turn back my hand against their oppressors."[463]

But that doesn't mean that we can just ignore the battle. In the Book of Revelation, in the warnings to the Churches, the City of Laodicea was condemned because it was neither cold nor hot. It was lukewarm. As a result, the Lord said, "I will spit you out of my mouth."[464] Laodicea was rich and affluent. They did not feel that they needed anything. And yet they were condemned as being truly poor in the only things that really matter. We cannot be lukewarm.

Sitting on the sidelines just gives aid to the enemy, and the consequences of this battle are enormous. Hell is a horrible place, and it is forever. As St. Thomas Aquinas tells us in his "Thanksgiving After Mass," Heaven is the place where all of our real dreams and desires will be satisfied beyond our wildest

---

461 John 15:5.
462 2. Cor. 12:9.
463 Psalm 81:14-15. See also Psalm 44:4 and Isaiah 48:18.
464 Rev. 3:15-16.

imagination. That is what we are fighting about, not only for ourselves, but for all those we love. To put it another way, we are engaged in a battle for the eternity of our loved ones.

Edmund Burke was an English politician in the 1700s who supported the American Revolution (not a very popular thing to do at the time). He once said, "The only thing necessary for the triumph of evil is for good men to do nothing." We must join in the battle.

And we should not be timid and defensive in our engagement. Once I read a reflection by Bishop Robert Barron in the *Magnificat* where he commented on Christ's promise to St. Peter at Caesarea Philippi.[465] Peter had just proclaimed Jesus the Christ, the Son of God. Jesus said, "And so I say to you, you are Peter, and upon this rock I will build my church, and the gates of the netherworld shall not prevail against it."

Bishop Barron admitted that he had misunderstood this passage for most of his life, and I think that all of us have too. In the ancient world, the wall of a city was its ultimate defense against an attacking army. Jesus did not say that the gates of the Church would withstand an attack by Hell. He said that the gates of Hell would not be able to withstand the assault of the Church. We must be on the offensive. But it is an offensive unlike anything we know in our world.

In a sense, we are called to engage in spiritual guerrilla warfare, attacking from the fringe and then disappearing into the surrounding area to let God, our Champion, fight the actual battle. But we are called to foster a kind of a spiritual revolution.

---

465 *Magnificat*, August 2017, Vol. 19, No. 6, p. 376.

There is an old Latin hymn, the *Laudes Regiae*, that includes the following lyric:

Christus vincit!

Christus regnat!

Christus imperat!

In English,

Christ conquers;

Christ reigns;

Christ commands.

In the end, Christ Wins. The forces of Hell cannot prevail against our all-powerful God.

I would like to conclude this Handbook with a quote from another ancient hymn. The *Te Deum* is traditionally attributed to Sts. Augustine and Ambrose. It is a hymn of praise that is sung on all of the major feast days in the Office of the Church, the Liturgy of the Hours. It concludes with the following line which I think is appropriate for us today:

In te, Dómine, sperávi:

Non confúndar in ætérnum.

One English translation is as follows:

"In You, oh Lord, is our hope,

And we shall never hope in vain."

So pray; live a life of selfless love (holiness); and unite your sufferings to the Cross of Christ. And leave the rest up to God.

God bless and prosper you and yours.

Appendix A

THE ROSARY

Although the Rosary is viewed as a Marian devotion, it is also designed to help us to grow closer to the significant events of Our Lord during his life. That is why we have the mysteries, as follows (with Scriptural references):

The Joyful Mysteries

- *The Annunciation* - Luke 1:26-38
- *The Visitation* - Luke 1:39-56
- *The Nativity* - Luke 2:1-14 and ff.
- *The Presentation* - Luke 2:22-38
- *The Discovery of Jesus in the Temple* - Luke 2:41-51

The Luminous Mysteries

- *The Baptism of Our Lord* - Matt. 3:13-17, Mark 1:9-11, Luke 3:21-22, John 1:31-34
- *The Wedding at Cana* - John 2:1-11
- *The Proclamation of the Kingdom* - Mark 1:15
- *The Transfiguration* - Matt. 17:1-8, Mark 9:2-8, Luke 9:28-36, Peter 1:16-18

- *The Institution of the Eucharist* - Matt. 26:17-35, Mark 14:22-31, Luke 22:14-38, John 13:1-17:26

The Sorrowful Mysteries
- *The Agony in the Garden* - Matt. 26:36-46, Mark 14:32-42, Luke 22:39-46
- *The Scourging at the Pillar* - Luke 23:16, John 19:1
- *The Crown of Thorns* - Matt. 27:27-31, Mark 15:16-20, John 19:2
- *Jesus is Made to Bear His Cross* - Matt. 27:32, Mark 15:21, Luke 23:26-32, John 19:17
- *The Crucifixion* - Matt. 27:33-56, Mark 15:22-41, Luke 23:33-49, John 19:17-37

The Glorious Mysteries
- *The Resurrection* - Matt. 28:1-10, Mark 16:1-8, Luke 24:1-12, John 20:1-18
- *The Ascension* - Acts 1:6-12
- *Pentecost* - Acts 2:1-41
- *The Assumption* - Psalm 16:10
- *The Coronation of Mary* - Revelation 12:1

Appendix B

ADDITIONAL PRAYERS

Prayer of St. Alphonsus When Visiting a Chapel

My LORD Jesus Christ, Who because of Your love for men remain night and day in the Blessed Sacrament, full of pity and of love, awaiting, calling and welcoming all who come to visit You, I believe that You are present here on the altar. I adore You, and I thank You for all the graces You have bestowed on me, especially for having given me Yourself in this Sacrament, for having given me Your most holy Mother Mary to plead for me, and for having called me to visit You in this church.

I now salute Your most loving Heart, and that for three ends: first, in thanksgiving for this great gift; secondly, to make amends to You for all the outrages committed against You in this Sacrament by Your enemies; thirdly, I intend by this visit to adore You in all the places on earth in which You are present in the Blessed Sacrament and in which You are least honored and most abandoned.

My Jesus, I love You with my whole heart. I am very sorry for having so many times offended Your infinite goodness. With the help of Your grace, I purpose never to offend You again. And now, unworthy though I am, I consecrate myself to You without reserve. I renounce and give entirely to You my will, my affection, my desires and all that I possess. For the future, dispose of me and all I have as You please.

All I ask of You is Your holy love, final perseverance and that I may carry out Your will perfectly. I recommend to You the souls in Purgatory, especially those who had the greatest devotion to the Blessed Sacrament and to the Blessed Virgin Mary. I also recommend to You all poor sinners.

Finally, my dear Saviour, I unite all my desires with the desires of Your most loving Heart; and I offer them, thus united, to the Eternal Father, and beseech Him, in Your name and for love of You, to accept and grant them.

St. Alphonsus Liguori

Aquinas Prayer Before Mass

Almighty and ever-living God,
I approach the sacrament
of Your only-begotten Son
Our Lord Jesus Christ,
I come sick to the doctor of life,
unclean to the fountain of mercy,
blind to the radiance of eternal light,
and poor and needy to the Lord
of heaven and earth.

Lord, in your great generosity,
heal my sickness,
wash away my defilement,
enlighten my blindness, enrich my poverty,
and clothe my nakedness.

May I receive the bread of angels,
the King of kings and Lord of lords,
with humble reverence,
with the purity and faith,
the repentance and love,
and the determined purpose
that will help to bring me to salvation.
May I receive the sacrament
of the Lord's Body and Blood,
and its reality and power.

Kind God,
may I receive the Body
of Your only-begotten Son,
our Lord Jesus Christ,
born from the womb of the Virgin Mary,
and so be received into His mystical body
and numbered among His members.

Kind God, may I receive the Body
of Your only-begotten Son,our Lord Jesus Christ,
born from the womb of the Virgin Mary,
and so be received into His mystical body
and numbered among His members.

Loving Father, as on my earthly pilgrimage
I now receive Your beloved Son
under the veil of a sacrament,
may I one day see him face to face in glory,
who lives and reigns with You forever.

  St. Thomas Aquinas

Aquinas Prayer of Thanksgiving

Lord, Father all-powerful and ever-living God, I thank You, for
even though I am a sinner, your unprofitable servant, not because of my worth but in the kindness of your mercy, You have
fed me with the Precious Body and Blood of Your Son,
our Lord Jesus Christ.

I pray that this Holy Communion may not bring me
condemnation and punishment but forgiveness and salvation.

May it be a helmet of faith and a shield of good will.

May it purify me from evil ways and put an end to
my evil passions.

May it bring me charity and patience, humility and obedience,
and growth in the power to do good.

May it be my strong defense against all my enemies, visible and
invisible, and the perfect calming of all my evil impulses,
bodily and spiritual.

May it unite me more closely to you, the One true God, and lead
me safely through death to everlasting happiness with You. And

I pray that You will lead me, a sinner [and my entire family], to the banquet where you, with Your Son and Holy Spirit, are true and perfect light, total fulfillment, everlasting joy, gladness without end, and perfect happiness to your saints. Grant this through Christ our Lord, Amen.

St. Thomas Aquinas

Come, Holy Spirit

Come Holy Spirit,
fill the hearts of your faithful
and kindle in them the fire of your love.
Send forth your Spirit and they shall be created.
And You shall renew the face of the earth.

O, God, who by the light of the Holy Spirit,
did instruct the hearts of the faithful,
grant that by the same Holy Spirit
we may be truly wise and ever enjoy His consolations,

Through Christ Our Lord,

Amen.

Prayer for Inspiration from the Holy Spirit

O God, send forth your Holy Spirit into my heart that I may perceive, into my mind that I may remember, and into my soul that I may meditate.

Inspire me to speak with piety, holiness, tenderness, and mercy.

Teach, guide, and direct my thoughts and senses from beginning to end.

May your grace ever help and correct me, and may I be strengthened now with wisdom from on high, for the sake of your infinite mercy. Amen.

St. Anthony of Padua

Prayer to St. Michael the Archangel

St. Michael the Archangel,
defend us in battle.
Be our defense against the wickedness and snares of the Devil.
May God rebuke him, we humbly pray,
and do thou, O Prince of the heavenly hosts,
by the power of God,
thrust into hell Satan,
and all the evil spirits,
who prowl about the world
seeking the ruin of souls. Amen.

Pope Leo XIII

Guardian Angel Prayer

Angel of God,
my guardian dear,
To whom God's love
commits me here,
Ever this day,
be at my side,

To light and guard,
Rule and guide.

Amen.

The Franciscan Prayer

Lord, make me an instrument of your peace:
where there is hatred, let me sow love;
where there is injury, pardon;
where there is doubt, faith;
where there is despair, hope;
where there is darkness, light;
where there is sadness, joy.

O divine Master, grant that I may not so much seek
to be consoled as to console,
to be understood as to understand,
to be loved as to love.
For it is in giving that we receive,
it is in pardoning that we are pardoned,
and it is in dying that we are born to eternal life.

Amen.

Anima Christi

Soul of Christ, sanctify me
Body of Christ, save me
Blood of Christ, inebriate me
Water from Christ's side, wash me
Passion of Christ, strengthen me

O good Jesus, hear me
Within Your wounds hide me
Suffer me not to be separated from You
From the malicious enemy defend me
In the hour of my death call me
And bid me come unto You
That I may praise You with Your saints
and with Your angels
Forever and ever Amen

Jean-Baptiste Lully

Take, Lord, Receive

Take, Lord, and receive all my liberty,
my memory, my understanding,
and my entire will,
All I have and call my own.
You have given all to me.
To you, Lord, I return it.
Everything is yours; do with it what you will.
Give me only your love and your grace,
that is enough for me.

The Angelus

The Angel of the Lord declared to Mary:
And she conceived of the Holy Spirit.

Hail Mary...

Behold the handmaid of the Lord: Be it done unto me according
to Thy word.

Hail Mary . . .

And the Word was made Flesh: And dwelt among us.

Hail Mary . . .

Pray for us, O Holy Mother of God, that we may be made worthy of the promises of Christ.

Let us pray:
Pour forth, we beseech Thee, O Lord, Thy grace into our hearts; that we, to whom the incarnation of Christ, Thy Son, was made known by the message of an angel, may by His Passion and Cross be brought to the glory of His Resurrection, through the same Christ Our Lord.

Amen.

De Profundis

Out of the depths I cry to You, O Lord; Lord hear my voice. Let Your ears be attentive to the voice of my supplication. If You, O Lord, will mark iniquities, Lord, who shall stand it? For with You there is merciful forgiveness, and by reason of Your law, I have waited for You, O Lord. My soul has relied on His word, my soul hath hoped in the Lord. From the morning watch even until night, let Israel hope in the Lord. Because with the Lord there is mercy; and with Him plentiful redemption. And He shall redeem Israel from all his iniquities.
Amen

Acknowledgments

I need to thank and acknowledge certain people.

First, I want to thank my brain trust: Jon, Sam, Gene, Don, Bill, Dennis, Jeff, Eric, and Rob. These are the regulars of our Tuesday morning "bible study" group (we do start with a Bible passage, but we often go quickly off the rails after that). They have been very helpful in focusing topics for me and identifying discussion points for practicing Catholics. They point out when I am not making any sense which means that I need to rethink how I am saying something. I really appreciate their input.

I also want to thank Fr. Andrew Burkemper, one of our former parish priests. I asked for his help in making sure that I was properly stating the Church's position on various points. He has reviewed the manuscript a couple of times pointing out some phrasings that needed to be restated to avoid any confusion. He also helped to tweak the flow of the manuscript, pointing out where the text didn't flow as well as it could. He was very helpful.

Finally, I want to thank my editor, Katie Hall. She read the manuscript when it was very much of a work in progress, but she thought she saw some potential. She has reviewed it several times, suggesting restructuring certain sections to make them flow better. One of the humorous things that both she and Fr. Burkemper did early on was to tell me that I hadn't written enough on certain topics. She also helped to identify sections where I had failed to make my point. And since I had never written anything like this before, she convinced me to take my writing more seriously.

I owe a lot to her encouragement and her constructive criticism. I think that the manuscript improved tremendously under her watchful eye.

And thanks to John Fischer and Ed Crites who read a very early version of the manuscript and provided comments. I really appreciate everyone's help on this.

About the Author

Fred Vilbig lives in St. Louis, Missouri, where he and his wife raised their eleven children, sending them all to their local parish grade school. He is a graduate of the University of Dallas (B.A. in Philosophy, 1979) and St. Louis University School of Law (J.D., 1982). He was licensed in Missouri and is admitted to practice before the US Supreme Court. He practices law in Clayton, Missouri, where he works with small businesses and helps families with wills, trusts, and probate matters. He has been a periodic host of the Catholic radio program, St. Joseph Radio Presents, which previously aired on EWTN, but currently airs locally in St. Louis. He is an erstwhile speaker at local parishes (including his own) on various faith matters. He was the president of the St. Louis Catholic lawyers association, the St. Thomas More Society. He is a member of the Knights of Columbus, Knighthood Degree (formerly, Third Degree). He has served on his local city council and on various city boards, as well as on the boards of local, regional, and national nonprofit entities. He has taught numerous continuing education courses and has spoken to graduate classes in financial planning. He has also taught graduate classes in finance. He is the author of a local newspaper column, Law Matters, and an estate planning book, *You Can't Take It With You*, in addition to writing a blog on his website, www.law-matters.net.

CPSIA information can be obtained
at www.ICGtesting.com
Printed in the USA
BVHW070734110121
597460BV00001B/9